'April Holden works with th[...]
Operation Mobilisation's gl[...]
Us Love details April's comp[...]
to the human brokenness [...]

Effective training programmes for community, church, students and crisis care workers have been built around resources that have been successful in similar ministries. Crisis Care Training International is grateful for the opportunity to join hands with April Holden in her vision to continue God's story of binding up the broken-hearted and setting captives free. Readers will be challenged to join April in embracing this vision.'

Phyllis Kilbourn, PhD, Founder and Education Director,
Crisis Care Training International

'I am excited about this book about April Holden, one of our experienced missionaries. Africa is one of the continents that has faced numerous challenges, especially where loving one another is concerned. I am happy this book addresses this need, and hope many will be blessed by it.'

Melvin Chiombe, OM Africa Area Director

'Equal parts a call to compassion and a challenge to complacency, this book is a remarkable testimony to what God can do when you follow Him wholeheartedly.'

Andy Butcher, author of Street Children

They Called Us Love

The story of April Holden and Africa's street children

Deborah Meroff

First published in Great Britain in 2018

Society for Promoting Christian Knowledge
36 Causton Street
London SW1P 4ST
www.spck.org.uk

British Library Cataloguing-in-Publication Data
A catalogue record for this book is available from the British Library

ISBN 978–0–281–07906–3
eBook ISBN 978–0–281–07907–0

1 3 5 7 9 10 8 6 4 2

Typeset by Falcon Oast Graphic Art Limited
First printed in Great Britain by Jellyfish Print Solutions
Subsequently digitally reprinted in Great Britain

eBook by Falcon Oast Graphic Art Limited

Produced on paper from sustainable forests

This book is dedicated to the children and young people who still struggle to survive on the streets of our world, waiting for love and waiting for hope; also to the boys at the Centres of Love who have grown into fine men of God

Author's note

———◦——

'April Holden' is a pen name for use in sensitive countries where ongoing Christian ministries may be at risk. For this reason, place names and other identifying details have also been omitted or changed, as well as the names of individuals, in Chapters 3 to 10 of this book.

Contents

Foreword

One of the most important messages I have preached during my last half-century of missions involvement concerns 'seven people lying at the side of the road', based on the parable of the Good Samaritan. I believe this is a fitting message for us today because there are so many marginalized people who are suffering and needing Jesus – both for salvation and for those practical, life-sustaining requirements we all have. At the same time, it has been my great joy to see, within Operation Mobilisation (OM), a huge shift in recent years towards marrying gospel proclamation and social action.

These 'seven people' – who, by the way, I also list on the back of my business card as a constant reminder – are (1) children at risk, (2) abused women, (3) the extreme poor, (4) HIV and AIDS patients, (5) people with impure water, (6) the unborn and (7) the environmentally impacted.

UNICEF has estimated that 100 million children worldwide fit under the single category of 'kids on the streets'. Other children at risk include those who are orphaned by AIDS or living in slums and around rubbish dumps; victims of sex trafficking, domestic abuse or slave labour; and child soldiers.

If we don't help them, who will? This is the question a young British woman named April Holden asked herself and then answered by devoting her life to Africa's homeless children. April was not a likely candidate to sign up for such an assignment. She had so many physical health difficulties that she was turned down by the first mission she applied to and told that going to Africa would lead to her death. Yet she went anyway, in obedience to God, and pioneered homes for street boys in one of the most difficult war-torn countries in North Africa.

When April was suddenly deported from that nation after 17 years, God recommissioned her to initiate an Africa-wide ministry for OM. Hope on the Streets for Children, based in Zambia, is now helping to mobilize African churches to change the lives of thousands of vulnerable children.

'Responsibility' is an interesting word when you take it apart. Most of us have the ability to respond to people in need in some way, even if we are not wealthy or healthy, but do we feel the urgency to respond? Zechariah 7.8–10 makes God's view on the matter very clear: 'This is what the LORD Almighty said: "Administer true justice; show mercy and compassion to one another. Do not oppress the widow or the fatherless, the foreigner or the poor."'

The bottom line is that the fatherless are on God's heart. Let's keep His passion in mind as we read the pages of this book. And then let us respond!

George Verwer
Founder, Operation Mobilisation (OM International)

Preface

Many people say to me, 'Oh, you have done a great work!' or something similar. In reality, I have played just a small part. I have coordinated activities, trained people and done a lot of administration. In North Africa, the 35-plus staff members of our Centres of Love were the real heroes, living with the children day in, day out. They handled the lion's share of the ministry in the boys' centres. As a family, we were totally dependent on one another's different skills and personalities, and encouraged each other whenever we were weak. Each one of us played our part: some small, some great. We all made mistakes. Yet, in spite of our failings God used us.

In reality, it is God Himself whom we celebrate in this book. He alone deserves the honour and glory for transforming the lives of the children we have worked with. Throughout Africa the Father of the fatherless has taken our five loaves and two fish and multiplied them to do things beyond anything we could imagine. So we do not take credit. We only want to give thanks for the tremendous privilege of being allowed to serve alongside our Lord to rescue more than 300 children in one country alone from a virtual dead end on the streets. Together we welcomed these lost boys to a loving family here on earth, as well as the anticipation of an eternal family. For over 17 years, He faithfully provided food, education, supplies, salaries and emergency needs at our Centres of Love. The children never went without and, to our knowledge, against all the odds, all but six of our boys grew up to be men of God. Such results defy logic.

Today that same God continues to direct and sustain us in our new vision, which is to mobilize and train His Church to rescue children all over Africa. This continent has 33 million children and young people who live on the streets. Yet it is also home to 542 million Christians. Since the Church is a family headed by God the Father, doesn't it make sense for His people also to serve as the family to the fatherless? My passion is to prepare men and women to act as facilitators alongside African churches and communities, so they can reach out to the homeless in a godly, professional and sustainable manner.

In closing, I'd like to reaffirm that God delights in using even the most unlikely or unqualified of us on His rescue team.

> Brothers and sisters, think of what you were when you were called. Not many of you were wise by human standards; not many were influential; not many were of noble birth. But God chose the foolish things of the world to shame the wise; God chose the weak things of the world to shame the strong.   (1 Corinthians 1.26–27)

To God be the glory.

April Holden

Acknowledgements

I, 'April', want to acknowledge the many colleagues who have worked or are presently working alongside me to make our vision to help vulnerable children a reality, as well as our partners and support workers all over the world – each of us fulfilling the role that God has given us. I thank all friends and family who have tirelessly stood by me all these years. Lastly, I thank Debbie Meroff for all the hard work she has put into writing this story.

Prologue

———◆———

'Fear not . . . I have called you by name, you are mine.'
(Isaiah 43.1, ESV)

The day April had been dreading for so many months was finally
here. A message had been left by a government security officer while
she was busy in her classroom, teaching. When April returned the
call, she was ordered to report in person at nine the next morning.
In turmoil, and fully expecting to be given only 48 hours to leave the
country like her friends and co-workers, she spent most of the night
packing and making plans. Keeping herself very busy helped; that
way she didn't have a chance to think beyond what she was doing.
Early in the morning she called an urgent meeting of the ministry
staff to inform them of what was happening. Privately, she told her
close friend Esther that she might never see her again.

Ever since this North African country had declared a one-religion
(Islam) and one-culture and language (Arabic) policy, Christians
had been made to feel unwelcome. Thousands had fled south. Others
had been attacked, churches and Christian organizations closed.
Security forces often picked up foreign and national believers for
questioning. Some of her friends had been released after only a day
or two; others were still in prison. Although everyone tried to carry
on with their routines as normally as possible, the tension was escalating, becoming unbearable.

By ordering April to report to the national security office rather
than escorting her directly to prison, officials had neatly circum-
vented the British embassy's right to be involved. When she walked
inside the grim building the next morning, she was directed to sit on
a hard chair in the reception area. This L-shaped room was already
crowded with an assortment of other individuals. Mostly these were
foreigners, but April's heart fell as she saw that members of her staff
had also been called in, including Esther. Armed guards ensured

that none of the detainees spoke to each other or moved as, one by one, they were summoned upstairs for interrogation.

April had to return to the office for the next nine days, sitting there for 10 to 15 hours during the first sessions, and then about 10 hours. Her turn for questioning came once or twice a day, sometimes for only an hour or less at a time. The guards allowed no respite from the painful hours of sitting, except for occasional toilet breaks. She spent much of the time silently talking with God, sensing His presence. On Sunday, when there was only one guard and he stepped out of the reception area, everyone present immediately exchanged whispered songs, prayer and Bible verses, encouraged by an elderly pastor. At midnight or one in the morning, she and the others were allowed to return home for a few hours.

She was thankful for this as the precious interval allowed her to communicate with the embassy, friends and family. But as the week dragged on, with little sleep and she faced the repeated hammering of her interrogator, she felt increasingly fragile. Her mind and body ached with weariness, her stomach churned and she felt feverish. Far worse than the physical discomfort was the dread that coiled inside her every time she thought of the sentence that seemed inevitable. Would it be prison – or permanent banishment from all that she had loved and worked for?

Upstairs in the small interrogation room, the officer faced April from behind a desk. At first he accused her of lying. Then he attempted to manipulate her with bizarre behaviour, sometimes smiling in a friendly, beguiling manner and at other times shouting, his features contorted with anger. Once the man even gave her a few hours to go and say goodbye to the boys at the centre. It was agonizing. She only had time to gather a few of the children, along with some staff members. They were all very upset at the loss of their Mama April. She was determined not to let herself cry, but when she tried to talk to them, her throat closed up.

Obviously her interrogator wanted her to implicate other people in her 'crime' of redeeming vulnerable children, but she refused to give him any names. Eventually, Esther and her other co-workers were released. As long as she could concentrate on the reality of her all-powerful God, April managed to remain calm. 'Greater is He who is within you than he who is in the world', she reminded herself, over and over.

Each night April opened her Bible and drew comfort from the promises it held. She had claimed verse 9 of the first chapter of Joshua back when she took her first step into missions: 'Have I not commanded you? Be strong and courageous. Do not be afraid; do not be discouraged, for the LORD your God will be with you wherever you go.' Although her interrogator repeatedly threatened her with prison, she felt an inward certainty that the Lord would not ask this of her.

Sometimes, as the days and nights ran into each other, her exhausted mind drifted from her present circumstances. She let herself retrace the astonishing path she had followed to this North African country . . . a journey that went back 20 years to the village of Rainford, on the outskirts of St Helens, England.

April's first major life crisis had occurred at the formative age of seven, when doctors discovered a lump in her oesophagus. Everyone feared the worst as her inability to swallow food led to severe weight loss. She was a desperately ill little girl. Then, mercifully, the lump was removed and a biopsy on her neck ruled out cancer. After a second operation was carried out to remove her appendix, April recuperated and life returned to normal.

Except another event happened about the same time. To April, regular church attendance had simply been part of her weekly routine. She believed that Jesus Christ was a real person who had lived and died, but so had other famous people in history. When she returned to church after her operations, one of the ladies there, Mrs Birchall, assured April that it was the Lord Jesus who had healed her. A light clicked on in her heart. Could it be that Jesus really wasn't dead, even though she couldn't see Him, and He cared enough about her to heal her, as small and unimportant as she was?

She thought about it. The next time the minister explained that God sent His only Son, Jesus Christ, to die a terrible death in her place, April listened carefully. She knew she hadn't done anything to deserve such an act of love – rather the opposite, in fact. She wanted to tell Jesus she was sorry He'd had to suffer so much for her sins.

At the close of that Sunday morning message April was ready.

'You gave me my life, and I give it back to You,' she whispered earnestly. 'I will do anything You want.'

Two years later, in Sunday school, April began to sense that God meant to take her up on that offer. She and the other children sat riveted as their teacher told them about a ministry that worked with destitute children in Bangladesh. She had never heard of Bangladesh and never been aware that such misery existed. Shouldn't she do something to help?

During a personal time of prayer that followed, April was sure that she heard the voice of God speak to her heart.

'You will work with homeless children in Africa,' the voice told her clearly.

Astonished but thrilled, April went home and told her mother what had happened.

'That's nice,' encouraged her mum. Though it was probably a passing fancy, she felt it reflected her daughter's tender spirit. But to April the revelation was real, and she never doubted it in all the years that followed, in spite of the roadblocks that threatened to deflect her from God's purpose.

Was her life's work now about to come to an end?

1

Painful beginnings

The LORD will fulfil his purpose for me; your steadfast love,
O LORD, endures for ever. Do not forsake the work of your hands.
(Psalm 138.8, ESV)

April Holden drew her first breath of a sweet English spring on 8 April 1963. The rundown neighbourhood where she and her older sister Susan started life in Parr, a suburb of St Helens, Lancashire,[1] was not so sweet. Two years later, their home was declared derelict. The family was forced to move to government-subsidized council housing in Thatto Heath, another suburb of St Helens.

When April became critically ill and gave her life to Jesus at the age of seven, it changed everything. Her Sunday school teachers and youth leaders were an important influence during the years that followed, as were members of her own family, most of whom were practising Christians. Relatives were in and out of each other's homes all the time, sharing Sunday meals after church and even enjoying holidays together.

As she grew older, April developed her interests in music, dancing, reading and swimming. Her IQ was above average, but she had to work hard for good grades because of an attention deficit hyperactivity disorder (ADHD) that triggered memory lapses. A tendency towards extreme timidity and nervousness led to stomach upsets and other frequent illnesses. All this left her with very low self-esteem. Fortunately, big sister Susan always kept a protective eye on her.

When April was 12, her father secured a better job with the bank and the Holden family moved from the urban outskirts of St Helens to the rural village of Rainford nearby. Leaving her old friends behind was hard, and her painful shyness was a barrier to making new ones. Worse, she found herself ridiculed at school for her 'common' accent. The fact that she took an eager interest in learning and her body was hopelessly uncoordinated when it came to sports involving controlling a ball didn't help her popularity. To top it off, she was the only girl in her year to attend Christian meetings at school. Some of the boys delighted in mocking her with shouts of 'God squad!' as she passed.

The constant bullying hurt, but perhaps it was the loneliness of April's teenage years that made her friendship with Jesus doubly precious. One day when she was 14 and alone in her room, giving in to her unhappiness, she suddenly experienced a breathtaking awareness of Jesus' presence. She had a clear vision of Him sitting beside her on her bed. Then, with fathomless depths of tenderness, He began gently to speak, assuring April that all would be well. She should never again feel alone or forgotten, He said, for He was always with her.

Awestruck by this evidence of God's concern for her situation, it didn't seem to matter so much after that when kids made fun of her. She even had confidence enough to laugh with them. Slowly, April's situation improved and she gained more friends.

During her teenage years, the near-constant physical pain April had begun to suffer was finally diagnosed as arthritis of the spine. This disease ran in her family, although it didn't usually affect someone so young. Later, doctors defined the particular form of arthritis in her back, neck and shoulders as spondylitis. The condition sometimes caused a pins-and-needles sensation followed by numbness; at other times she was attacked by agonizing muscle spasms. The arthritis also resulted in a herniated disc in her lumbar region, and bone spurs in her neck, which caused tingling or numbness in her hands. The disease, they told her, was degenerative. By the time she was in her late teens, her mobility was often limited. Later, the disease progressed to the point where April was unable to firmly grasp or lift objects.

After secondary school, April elected to attend university in Liverpool. Her high mock exam results, added to three summers of experience as a hospital volunteer, had prompted several offers of places at medical schools, but then her health broke down and her final exam results fell short of what was expected. April decided not to re-sit them and went into biochemistry instead. Later, drawn to the teaching profession, she altered her degree course to life sciences in order to have a wider field of study.

During her first year, April attended a talk by an Africa Inland Mission (AIM) missionary at her Christian Union. The hard facts and stories she heard about the world's desperate physical and spiritual hunger electrified her. Only 19, but determined to get her priorities straight, she applied to join AIM.

AIM's response left her crushed. April's chronic health problems did not make her a good candidate for missionary work and the agency stated this in no uncertain terms. She should not even consider going to Africa, because she would doubtless die. In their opinion April had mistaken God's direction. While she could certainly pray for Africa and support other missionaries, they concluded that she should never go there herself.

April was deeply disappointed. Since she had very little confidence in herself, however, she accepted the mission's verdict – at least for the time being.

That same year, a doctor at the university suggested April might have allergies that were contributing to her illnesses. By identifying these allergies and avoiding certain foods, she was able to stop taking the medication she had been prescribed for years. This was a tremendous encouragement.

In the meantime, God was using Spirit-filled Christians in April's church in Liverpool to make her reassess her spiritual health. Times of worship with these believers offered a whole new dimension to praise, and reflected a closer relationship with the Lord than she herself enjoyed. When she talked this over with her father, however, he discouraged her from having further contact with the group. He was afraid that they were fanatics – part of a sect. Although April sensed that they were not, but on the contrary possessed something she needed, she was too proud to confess this fact and probe deeper. After all, wasn't she a youth leader and Sunday school teacher, not to mention secretary of the university's Christian Union?

When April had completed her studies at Liverpool, the teacher training school told her that they didn't believe she had the physical and emotional stamina to start teaching full time. Taking a gap year might make sense, she decided, but refusing softer options, she accepted a post as a volunteer carer in a Methodist home in Ealing, London. Six severely disabled children lived in her unit and she was involved in their daily practical care, such as feeding, bathing, exercising, playing and giving them their therapy and so on. She also performed general cleaning and tidying duties. All but one of her charges were quadriplegic due to cerebral palsy, and one child was also deaf and blind. Another boy had cerebral palsy affecting his legs and a learning disability. Most of the six residents had an infant-level mental age.

In spite of the rigorous 60-hour-per-week schedule that demanded a great deal of hard work and sacrifice, April found the job very rewarding. Perhaps the hardest thing she faced during her time there was the death of one of the little girls in her particular care. All the same, the whole experience convinced April that even the most severely disabled child has personality and potential.

After a year, April went to college to qualify for her postgraduate Certificate of Education. This course would give her qualified teacher status, allowing her to get a job in England's state schools.

Unfortunately, during her time at the Methodist home April's emotional insecurities had led to an involvement with a much older man. The relationship, when it ended, left her devastatingly aware that she had taken a wrong turn. She despised herself for her weak faith and for disappointing the Lord after all He had done for her. Humbled and depressed she returned home, certain that she would never earn His forgiveness.

One day, April agreed to act on her mother's suggestion to attend a new Christian house fellowship that had recently started up. The group exposed her once again to men and women who were filled with God's Spirit, and this time her analytical mind drove her to ask questions until she found the truth. At first the others wondered if this newcomer simply had a critical attitude, but when they saw that she was sincerely seeking answers, they were happy to share what they had learned from the Scriptures. April was finally convinced that she needed to surrender her own will completely. She invited the Holy Spirit to take control of every aspect of her life.

It was a huge spiritual turning point. She now understood that no one can earn God's forgiveness. It is a free gift. The words of John 8.36 – 'So if the Son sets you free, you will be free indeed' – became a reality. As April experienced deliverance from many issues that had kept her from enjoying inner peace, her family marvelled at her newfound confidence. They could now accept that Christians who walk in the Spirit might be different, but they are certainly not a sect.

April accepted a teaching job back in Parr – the town where she had been born. Parr Flat Junior was a rather unusual pilot community school that offered education and involvement to parents during the evenings, weekends and holidays. In her classes she had a mixture of children ranging from genius level to a student who could speak only four words and hid under the table if she raised her voice. Some of the children were quite 'normal', while one was an elective mute; another loved to climb on to the roof and one boy was a compulsive arsonist!

During her two years of teaching at Parr, April found herself drawn to the special needs students among her seven- and eight-year-olds. Although she enjoyed her time there she was motivated to apply to Beacon School, established in Skelmersdale, Lancashire, about 20 minutes from her village. The emotionally disturbed children who attended Beacon had all been expelled twice from other schools for their violent behaviour; if they failed again they would have to go to a reform boarding school. As she was to discover, some of these 'write-offs' shouldn't have been at Beacon School at all, because they were autistic. One five-year-old was actually a genius who had simply been bored in ordinary schools. Most of the students came from broken homes or abusive situations.

April spent the next three years teaching ages four to seven at Beacon School, and another year and a half teaching ages 10 to 11. The intensive in-service training stretched her in every way and was to stand her in good stead in the years to come.

Driving to work one day during her fourth year at Beacon, the lyrics of a Dan Schutte worship song on her tape deck, 'Here I Am, Lord', suddenly grabbed April's attention. A profound conviction came over her. Then, just as it had over ten years earlier, God's voice spoke very clearly to April. This time the words held a gentle rebuke.

'I told you that I want you to go to Africa,' He said.

The reminder pierced April's heart like a sword. She could not deny that she had somehow lost her focus during the years of university studies and teaching. She was also convinced that the 'Lord of sea and sky' would not ask her again.

April took action, signing up to attend the UK's annual, countrywide Spring Harvest conference that year. Studying the many mission agency displays at this major Christian gathering, she decided to apply to them all, without specifying where she wanted to serve. Hopefully God would lead her to the right mission.

When one of them eventually accepted her application, however, April was afraid to explain that she felt called to Africa. What if they responded the same way as AIM had, years earlier? At the new recruits' conference in Germany that January 1993, however, the Lord definitely sealed her conviction that she should follow Him to Africa. Her research had exposed the tragedy of over 32 million children and young people who, through no fault of their own, were struggling to survive on the streets of that continent. There had to be something she could do about it, but which country exactly did God have in mind? Further prayer and study of resources such as *Operation World* (Mandryk, 2010) made her zero in on a war-ravaged North African country that had one of the highest numbers of internally displaced people on record.

Mission leaders talked with April and wisely suggested that she should first get her feet wet in Egypt. She had much to learn about Arab culture in Africa and would benefit from picking up some Arabic. At the same time, she could put her teaching skills to work in a small school in Cairo that had been established for the children of team members.

April at first resisted this proposal, not wanting to be diverted from the part of Africa that was most in her heart. The more she thought about it, though, the more she realized that Egypt could be part of God's perfect plan. He had been preparing her all along – almost in spite of herself – for her move into missions. Securing a university degree had not equipped her with all the credentials she needed for Africa, so He had seen to it that she acquired training and experience in dealing with physically and behaviourally damaged children.

Most importantly she had needed to reach the end of herself: a place of surrender where only God's Spirit could complete her as a person. Now she was able to see Egypt as a logical first step, introducing her to the mission world before moving on.

When April broke the news to her family, they were fully supportive.

'I wondered when you would get round to it,' her mum smiled, quietly satisfied. She had not forgotten the long-ago day when her small daughter had announced that she was going to work with homeless children in Africa – even though she had never mentioned it to April since or pushed her in that direction. Her parents and sister, as well as a number of her extended family, committed to supporting her financially. So did several churches, including the fellowship where she had given her life to the Lord and felt called to missions. St John's Ravenhead was to stand behind her through all her years in North Africa and raise money for projects; its people continue to pray for her even now. Her home church in Rainford also partnered with April. The pastor there only requested that she wait until they found people to replace her as the youth group leader and joint churches committee representative. He also had everyone's approval to appoint April as an elder in the church, telling her, 'You will be our elder doing missionary work overseas.'

The months before she left for Egypt flew by. In between sorting out possessions and deciding what she needed to take with her, April sent friends and churches a prayer and mission vision letter and accepted many invitations to speak.

April's doctor was obviously concerned about her ability to cope with allergies, the arthritis in her spine and frequent, painful back spasms. To her vast relief, however, he decided these problems were not likely to worsen in Egypt and so did not overrule her going.

On the day of her departure, April's family accompanied her to the airport to give her their last hugs and best wishes. She heard her parents' cry, 'We love you! Keep in touch!' and saw her mother fighting back tears as she passed through security. At last April boarded the plane that would take her out of her comfort zone for the rest of her life.

April had tears too, tears that were mixed with a deep feeling of joy. Despite all the uncertainties over what lay ahead, she held fast to the blessed assurance that the Lord, her Rock, would never leave her or forsake her. His enduring promise of 'Lo, I am with you always, even to the end of the age' (Matthew 28.20, NASB) was never more real.

2

Egypt: brave new world

———— ▸•◂ ————

'For I know the plans I have for you,' declares the LORD, 'plans
to prosper you and not to harm you, plans to give you hope and
a future.'   (Jeremiah 29.11)

As April's plane touched down on to the runway she was blinded by
the dazzle of sun and sand that rushed up to meet her. It was January
1993 and, against the odds, she had made it as far as Cairo.

April thought that she had prepared herself. She knew that Egypt
was 96 per cent desert, with rain falling only about five days of the
year. This meant that 95 per cent of the country's population crowded
along the life-giving Nile. Yet, until she came face to face with the
arid landscape, she had found it hard to grasp that Egyptians only
enjoyed an average of 18 square centimetres of greenery per person,
compared to the 17 square metres she had taken for granted back
home.

The Nile, she read, was the longest river on the planet. April
thought of it as a circulatory system through which Egypt's life had
flowed for 7,000 years, with Cairo at its heart. The city that had been
designed for only four million now throbbed with four times that
number – and was swelling by another million each year.

Through April's senses swirled a bewildering sandstorm of sights,
sounds and smells radically different from anything she had ever experienced before. As she emerged from the airport, the heat and dust
slammed into her; at the same time she was confronted with a cac-
ophony of crowded streets and the harsh cadence of spoken Arabic.
Could there be any greater contrast to life in a quiet English village?

Stretched on her bed that night, April lay listening to the cease-
less barking of dogs, blaring of traffic horns and shouts of passers-by

that floated through the open windows. After falling into a troubled sleep, she was jolted awake just before dawn as a terrific din erupted all over the city, steadily gathering momentum until it reached a crescendo: the 4 a.m. call to prayer.

The official start for every Muslim's first daily duty seemed to be a matter of dispute, for just as one mullah's chant ceased from the loudspeaker of a nearby mosque, another one took it up. No wonder Cairo was called 'the city of a thousand minarets'!

The prophet Muhammad's summons to believers rang out five times daily. Although the early morning call was the most difficult to adjust to, April eventually took it in her stride, along with the subsequent cries of men and boys selling produce in the streets. During the month of Ramadan, when Muslims observed a dawn to sunset fast, callers even passed through the streets to awaken everyone for breakfast at about 2 a.m.! The only time Cairo was ever really quiet was the 30 minutes before official sunset during that holiest of months. Then everyone was in their homes preparing food and eagerly waiting for their local mosque to give the all clear, so they could break their fast and begin a night of feasting.

Speaking of food, April was delighted to discover that the local cuisine posed no problem for her digestive system. Wealthy foreigners had access to speciality shops where they could buy familiar comfort foods, but this was not considered an option for workers committed to a sacrificial lifestyle. April enjoyed the brown bean stew called *ful* that was a staple in Egypt. She also liked falafel or *tamiya* (deep-fried balls of chickpeas and herbs), local salads and Egyptian flatbread, similar to pita.

Whenever she visited poorer areas, April prayed for God's protection of her health, knowing that she could not offend her hosts by refusing their food or drink. One day it occurred to her that she was trusting her heavenly Father to prevent stomach problems when she was outside her home, but she should be trusting Him at all times. So she came off her special diet, much to the alarm of the team nurse, who urged her to introduce only one new food at a time to her system.

'No. Either God has healed me or He hasn't!' she maintained, and thereafter took pleasure in trying a variety of new foods.

Adjusting to Cairo's climate was more difficult after a lifetime of English winters. Fortunately, the heat was less intense when she arrived in January than it would become during the summer months, when it soared to 42 °C (107 °F). Dust coated every surface, no matter how assiduous a person was at housekeeping. The city's air pollution index was the highest in the world – between 10 and 100 times more than acceptable levels. The sky overhead tended to be grey even on a clear day, though if one left the city limits it turned blue again.

Perhaps what was most astonishing was that many of the significant health issues that had plagued April before moving to Egypt no longer troubled her. In fact, she was to experience the complete healing of her allergies and asthma during her years in Cairo, despite the choking heat and dust. Only her arthritis persisted. The back pain was exacerbated, unfortunately, by once lifting a child the wrong way and not getting appropriate medical treatment.

Besides teaching on school days, April looked after 17 little ones under the age of seven during team days and retreats. Yet the Lord always gave her sufficient grace for the demands of each day.

April freely admitted that she was not a big-city girl. The fact that she was now forced to cope with one of the biggest and noisiest of the world's urban centres was enough to set off panic attacks. She cringed at her strange surroundings, reluctant at first to venture on her own through Cairo's narrow, rubbish-heaped streets. Pavements were usually usurped by cars double- or even triple-parked with brakes disengaged so they could, if necessary, be rolled out of the way. The tall buildings around her cut out the light. To see the sky she had to look straight up.

The city's efforts to accommodate rapid growth had resulted in a vast sprawl of slums that were home to 60,000 souls per 2.6 square kilometres or 1 square mile, compared to about 660 in Britain. The year before April's arrival, Egypt had suffered the most damaging earthquake in over 100 years, largely due to poor building codes of practice for high-rise apartments. Over 500 people had died and 50,000 were left homeless.

In fact, aftershocks were still shaking the city. Also, during her next year, Cairo was inundated by floods that turned streets into rivers. One day, a violent thunderstorm carried on for five hours, unleashing torrential rain and submerging the bottom floor of April and her flatmate Laura's four-storey apartment building, which they used for their school. The women scrambled to rescue whatever books they could and prevent further water damage.

Though Cairo was home to tens of thousands of foreigners, white Westerners stood out, especially those with light hair or blue eyes like April. She found most Egyptians to be friendly and disarmingly eager to try out their varying amounts of English. If they helped her with directions on the streets, they expected baksheesh. On the other hand, those who became genuine friends treated her like family.

April was, however, forced to come to terms with the fact that she could not enjoy the same casual friendliness with male acquaintances that she did at home. The first thing she was taught in her Arabic class was to shout '*Aiyb!*' – 'Shame!' – if a man on the street approached or spoke to her.

Women travelling on buses – even those accompanied by children – all too often faced the prospect of being pinched or groped by male passengers. After April suffered this indignity herself she learned to be careful and defensive at all times.

'You have to ignore men – act almost rude – or they may show up with gifts and ask you to marry them, even if they already have a wife and children!' advised one woman.

Once, when she was out showing a visitor around with a Christian friend named Mike, they met a stranger who asked if he could marry April. Mike was possessed of a wicked sense of humour and couldn't resist leading the man on. He urged the would-be bridegroom to make an offer of ten camels.

When the man finally agreed, Mike nodded. 'OK,' he said. 'I will speak to her father about it!'

Sometimes April used Cairo's metro system, which was quick and modern, with the names of stops written in English as well as Arabic. Tickets to any destination cost no more than the equivalent of 20 pence. To ensure propriety, the first carriage of each train was reserved exclusively for females.

April enjoyed studying her fellow passengers. Some women were swathed in traditional black from head to toe, the most conservative among them even covering their hands with thick black gloves. Clad in a light cotton dress herself, she was conscious of trickles of sweat running down her back in the airless compartment and could only imagine their discomfort. Schoolgirls and young women often wore a less severe, light-coloured kaftan or even a modest Western skirt and blouse with a white scarf covering their hair.

Girls in Egypt tended to marry young, since childbearing was considered the main purpose of womanhood. April was soon uncomfortably aware that single women – even married women without children – were accorded little respect. Only when a female gave birth to a (preferably male) child was she rewarded with the title of *Om* – 'mother of' – followed by the child's name.

In her book about Egyptian women, *Khul-Khaal* (1982), Nayra Atiya explains: '*Om* shows that a woman has fulfilled her calling, that of becoming a mother. Sometimes a childless woman will be called "*mother of the absent one*" in order not to use her first name, which would show disrespect or belittle her.'

One married lady April visited had been called '*Om*' for so long that she had forgotten her first name! Her world was closely constricted. From the day of her marriage onwards she had never wandered further than the street she lived on.

April had come to Cairo to teach students aged five to ten in a small school for the children of foreign team members opened and run by an American teacher called Laura Jenkins. Two of the children had special needs, so her former training was helpful. After working four and a half years in a school for emotionally and behaviourally disturbed students, April couldn't get over the fact that the little five-year-olds could read! She had lost sight of what was considered normal. She was also bemused when her class actually did what she asked the first time she spoke. It was like having Sunday school kids every day, she jested with Laura. That this school existed was critical, because it allowed the parents to fulfil their calling to live among and minister to the poorest of the poor. Altogether, there were 3 teachers and 16 children aged from 4 to 14.

Poverty was a grim fact of life for many in Cairo. Although the city boasted some 200,000 millionaires in the early 1990s, half of all the income generated went to only 5 per cent of its residents. Between the worlds of the very rich and very poor there was a great gulf.

The team April served was committed to learning Arabic and living at the same level as the destitute families in Muslim communities around them. In order to reach into their lives, only Jesus Christ and His cross could be a stumbling point between them and their neighbours.

'There's a deep rift between Muslim and Christian communities and it's not all to do with Jesus. It has to do with the clothes you wear, the food you eat and a lot of other things,' explained a leader. 'We ask God to change us until we don't refer to the poor as "they" but "we". We want to incarnate the gospel: wrap it up in ourselves and deliver it.'

April was deeply impressed by the sacrifices team members were willing to make. While she and Laura lived in a decent apartment used for the school, the slum buildings in which the other mission families lived often had no running water during the day, so most of their washing and cleaning had to be done at 11 or 12 at night, when water was available. Tough as the lifestyle was, they realized that there could be no short-cuts to earning the trust and friendship of their neighbours. Most were in it for the long haul.

As one of the wives shared, 'At first in our area we had rocks thrown at us because we are foreigners, and kids called us names. But not now. Now sometimes a woman says to me, "You're not like any foreigner I've ever seen. Why are you different?" To be invited into their lives, you have to prove your friendship. You must become vulnerable – cry with them, laugh with them. You can't just defend yourself all the time as a Christian to Muslims. They have many misconceptions. You must find things they believe that you also believe, and be patient. Show what God's love is. Without the Holy Spirit, it's impossible.'

Because this team worked exclusively among Muslims, they had little connection with Egyptian Christians. April was able to make good friends with the team members and helpers at Laura's school. She and Laura also regularly visited three Muslim ladies who were quite poor. They spent a lot of time with one in particular, a widow living with her daughter and one of her sons. The daughter was a long-time friend of Laura's who taught April Arabic one night a week, sometimes using the Bible. The mother always wanted to feed the girls and if they didn't eat enough to satisfy her she would cry, 'Eat! Eat! Don't you like my food?' So they learned to chew very slowly. Sadly, she was not very open to discussing spiritual things.

Another lady who lived in the poorest area also served food when they visited, even though she had so little. It would have been offensive to refuse. Years later, she actually gave her heart to Jesus. Although she was badly beaten, the woman refused to give up her faith and died a believer.

Most of the team members who lived in depressed areas of the city did not encourage other team members to visit them there. Too many foreigners attracted the wrong kind of attention. Social inter-action in the team was therefore limited to meetings, typically one day a week, when everyone got together for prayer, ministry and a little relaxation. Even then, however, April spent more time with the team kids than their parents. She loved being with them – in fact, she felt more comfortable with the little ones than with adults. Often (when her back was up to it) she held one child in each arm. Friends who found her alone at a retreat sometimes teased, 'What's wrong, April? Your arms are empty!'

The team was very pastoral and caring, however. When the leader noticed April's lack of self-esteem and tendency to shy away from interaction with adults, she provided counsel that helped her find confidence through her identity in Christ. A closer relationship to God led her to closer relationships with people around her too.

Twice-a-year retreats at the Red Sea provided much-needed get-aways for everyone. The first time April travelled south was on her thirtieth birthday. When they made a rest stop along the way, the team filled the bus with balloons and broke out a delicious array of multinational treats, serenading April with a rousing chorus of 'Happy Birthday'. After reaching their destination, she and Grace (a child travelling on another bus who had just turned five) enjoyed another birthday celebration. April's greatest thrill, however, was snorkelling in the colourful coral reefs of the Red Sea – an unforget-table introduction to God's underwater creation.

An occasional felucca[2] sail on the Nile or horseback jaunts into the desert with Laura also offered a break. How blissfully peaceful it was to ride with the pyramids behind them and the desert stretching ahead! The term 'ride' is used loosely as April had never taken formal riding lessons. She had to rely on the man at the stables to show her the basics – how to avoid falling off and how to turn her mount. Fortunately, she was assigned a quiet horse that was content to follow in Laura's horse's wake, for the most part. One day, however, her usually compliant mare must have been feeling frisky, for to April's chagrin she suddenly took off at full gallop in the wrong direction. Mercifully, April succeeded in hanging on until the animal ran out of steam. Once the mare was made to turn and caught sight of Laura's horse, she happily trotted back.

On another excursion, Laura and April stopped to visit a foreign friend on their way to the stables. She forgot to take off her earrings before climbing on to her horse, and realized later that she had lost one at some point during her ride. This was upsetting, because the jewellery had belonged to April's mother, who had passed away earlier that year. Knowing she could do nothing about it herself, she committed the loss to her heavenly Father. When she and Laura got back to the stables on the edge of the desert, they dismounted. There in the sand directly in front of her was the missing earring.

Whenever friends and family visited team members in Egypt it gave them the chance to take them to the pyramids, Giza's Pharaonic Village with all its living history, and other tourist attractions they didn't usually have time for. April was very pleased when her aunt, sister and brother-in-law arrived for two weeks in May 1996. The family took a one-day Nile cruise that created special memories for them all.

The unexpected loss of April's beloved mother during her second year in the field had been devastating. Her death seemed even worse because her mum's heart attack was a freak reaction to an injection during the course of a routine hospital procedure. Heartbroken, April had returned home for three months. She felt the burden of trying to be the strong one in the family, as everyone expected, but she and her mother had been very close. Her father also took the loss of his wife very badly. It was difficult for her to leave him to return to Egypt, but he urged her not to give up her work because of him.

C. S. Lewis (1996) had once written of his own bereavement:

With my mother's death all settled happiness, all that was tranquil and reliable, disappeared from my life. There was to be much fun, many pleasures, many stabs of joy; but no more of the old security. It was sea and islands now; the great continent had sunk like Atlantis.

For April, the great gap in her life meant learning to lean even harder on her heavenly Father.

Developing deep relationships with local people was, of course, restricted by April's lack of proficiency with the language. While many team members devoted much of their first year in the field to learning Arabic, April had needed to get straight into teaching each afternoon. Only her mornings and the summer break were devoted to intensive study of colloquial Arabic during her first six months. After that she taught full time.

As a student in England, April had struggled with learning languages; she had concluded that she was more of a scientist than a linguist. 'God,' she implored now, 'if I am to learn Arabic I need the gift of languages!' Within that first half year, she found that she was able to pick up a satisfying number of conversational skills, even though she had not yet learned to laugh at her mistakes. She complained that she spoke broken Arabic with an English 'accident' rather than accent!

On one mortifying occasion April asked her hostess for a bowl of socks (*surab*) instead of soup (*surba*). Thanks to Laura's patience as translator, however, April was able to make some good friends early on.

Egypt's Christian roots ran deep, its people introduced to the gospel of Jesus Christ early in the first century through the disciple Mark. Islam didn't arrive on the scene for six more centuries, but when it came, it conquered. While April lived in Egypt, the government was officially secular, but the law punished anyone who 'offended' Islam with five years in prison. Those who attempted to convert a Muslim could receive a three-year sentence. Every Christian congregation had at least two or three informers. Churches could be – and were – closed overnight, without explanation.

The growing prominence of fundamentalist Islam made security a serious concern for the team. Most expatriates knew that their phones were tapped. They received post only once a month by courier and they could not tell acquaintances, either Egyptian or foreign, that they were with a mission. April found the limitations on what she could and couldn't say very difficult.

Sometimes during her three and a half years in Cairo, April stood on her apartment balcony looking at the thousands of buildings surrounding her, counting at least 30 pencil-thin minarets piercing the sky in each direction. It was the people here who most caught at her heart: men, women and children who had no chance to hear that Jesus gave His life for them. It was for the sake of the children, in particular, that she had come this far and it was because Jesus had said 'Go!' that she was determined to take the next step.

Although God had used her time in Egypt to bless the children she taught, April knew her years there were really about preparing her for what lay ahead. She had grown emotionally and spiritually and, despite the fact that she had ended up spending more time in this country than anticipated, she now felt ready for an even deeper move into the Muslim world. Her certainty that she would be following God's direction in this never wavered.

One night in her sleep she was caught up in a very vivid dream. She found herself in a shelter where many dozens of dark-skinned boys were being loved and cared for. Instinctively she knew they were street boys and that the Father was giving her a glimpse into the future.

During a preliminary visit to her target country in March 1996, April went to see a street boys' centre run by Serving in Mission (SIM). Walking through the neighbourhood where she was staying, she felt a strange sense of coming home. Suddenly, as she toured the centre, she remembered the dream she had had some time before. A tingle of excitement travelled down her spine. This was the very place!

God has shown me the next step, she thought with wonder. *Why should I hesitate any longer?*

3

A cry in the night

Cry out in the night, as the watches of the night begin;
pour out your heart like water in the presence of the LORD.
Lift up your hands to him for the lives of your children,
who faint from hunger at every street corner.

(Lamentations 2.19)

April returned to Egypt with her heart full of anticipation. God seemed to be parting her personal Red Sea.

An invitation then came to teach two and a half days each week at the international school in the capital city of the country she was called to, allowing her an all-important work visa to live there. With all the arrangements falling into place, April flew from Cairo to the capital in August 1996. She was 33 years of age, ready at last to start the work God had called her to 24 years earlier.

What a relief to know He was in control! She was about to pioneer a ministry without the advantage of leadership training or experience in project design. Nor did she have a mentor at this point to steer her past the obstacles that would surely lie in her path. As April herself later put it, she simply put her foot on the tarmac and ran for the next 17 years.

April's part-time teaching job had not only opened the door to residency but it also eased her transition from the Egyptian culture. Volunteering at the SIM street children's centre a few days each week was another valuable learning experience. She hoped that first-hand observation of the local staff as they interacted with the boys would make her more 'streetwise'.

Transplanting here was not as much of a culture shock as it had been moving from England to Egypt, but it still called for major adjustments. Whereas Cairo had seemed to April more of a Middle Eastern culture, her new country of residence plunged her into the heart of Africa. The capital city was more spread out – and the pace more relaxed – than it was in Cairo. Only the main roads were paved, and surfaces were badly potholed. Camels, rickshaws and donkey carts shared the streets with ancient, broken-down cars and lorries converted into buses, with a scattering of modern vehicles thrown into the mix.

One of the first things that struck April was the number of homeless people sleeping on the edges of many roads, even on central reservations and roundabouts. She was also shocked to see lepers openly sitting outside the international school where she worked. In many ways it was as though she had travelled back in time. She could watch fishermen on the great river cast nets from feluccas, and farmers using hand-ploughs to till land alongside the river, just as their forefathers had for thousands of years.

The country's infrastructure was obviously less developed than Egypt's. The electricity supply was erratic at best, forcing residents to manage for days without power and water. When electricity was available, 12-hour cuts could be expected. Shopping also posed challenges. Many basic items were rationed for April's first couple of years there.

The climate too was hotter and drier than she had previously experienced, often reaching 42 °C (over 107 °F) and sometimes a sizzling 52 °C (125 °F). April was thankful that, although society was dominated by Islam, it was acceptable for her to wear long skirts and modest blouses that covered her shoulders. Black African women, whether Muslim or Christian, generally wore a *tob*, a length of material wrapped around the body that covered the head as well. Men tended to wear a light-coloured *jalabiya* (a floor-length traditional Arab garment), an African tunic with trousers or else Western clothes.

For the first several years, April shared a house designated for the mission's female team members. Having lived with only Laura in her Cairo apartment, April found living with four girls from four different countries and cultures, all with differing personalities and expectations, was not ideal. April was still by her own admission a people pleaser, so it was hard to keep all of her housemates happy all of the time. Also, they kept changing. Just as she got used to the likes and dislikes of one girl, another took her place.

Non-missionaries often give little thought to the complexities of accommodation in the field. Unlike married couples, single people seldom get to choose roommates or housemates; they are expected to adjust to strangers with whom they may have little in common. This can turn out to be extremely stressful, since these new recruits are wrestling simultaneously with a strange language, food and customs. Opposite personalities may generate resentments that, even though stifled, prompt feelings of guilt and failure on the part of new missionaries.

Unsurprisingly, after about five years of sharing close quarters, April embraced the opportunity to move into a place of her own that adjoined the girls' house, owned by the same landlady. She and Tanta Nirgis developed a close relationship. Tanta's husband also looked after the girls' welfare and one of the couple's sons was a fellow team member, very much like a brother to April. So she spent a lot of time with the whole extended family. Tanta Nirgis fondly referred to her as 'daughter' and whenever she was ill cosseted her with meals of stuffed pigeons, chicken soup and tea.

Sadly, Tanta's husband died during those first years and, not so long afterwards, so did April's beloved landlady. After moving to her third house, however, April was blessed to meet another very kind landlady. Mama Ferial had a son and daughter who lived in Australia and another son, blind from the age of 18, who lived with her. Mama was a devout Coptic Christian. She gave April the same loving care as Tanta Nirgis had and often took her adopted daughter a plate of food when she heard her coming home. The whole family has now emigrated to Australia, but April remains in touch.

After several years, a puppy named Lady bounded into April's heart and home. The dog proved to be a happy companion for the next nine years, affording plenty of light relief. She quickly caught on to her mistress's habit of rising at 5 a.m. for an hour of devotions before leaving for work. From then on, Lady woke April promptly at five each morning, whether or not it was a work day. With head down and hindquarters in the air, tail wagging enthusiastically, she made it clear it was playtime.

April considered her new country a friendly place. The streets were safer to walk along than in Cairo. Men were respectful and the people she met had a natural warmth. Only a few were hostile to foreigners. She grew used to hearing pedestrians calling '*khawaga*' – 'white foreigner!' – when she passed. She was told that the literal origin of the word meant 'the money came' and used to be applied to white foreigners as they were assumed to be wealthy. Asians were generally called Chinese, regardless of where they came from.

Residents were highly relational. It was important to greet people properly and take time to answer questions – which nobody, she noticed, was shy about asking. Among the top ten were 'Where are you from?', 'What are you doing in a North African country?' and, of course, 'Will you marry me?'

The 30 million or more people who lived in the country represented hundreds of different ethnic groups, all speaking diverse languages. April was pleasantly surprised that many who lived in the capital city knew at least a smattering of English, and she had no problem communicating with her Egyptian Arabic. In fact, to her amusement, her accent often convinced acquaintances that she was Egyptian. A typical conversation went like this:

'Which part of Egypt are you from?'

'I am from the UK.'

'Yes, but you grew up in Egypt.'

'No, I grew up in the UK.'

A confused look was followed by, 'Yes, but where did you learn Arabic?'

'In Egypt!'

'Ah, yes,' they would conclude, nodding. 'You are British, but you went to school in Egypt!'

Whereupon April gave up and simply smiled.

Three particular Arabic words, she soon discovered, were indispensable in daily conversation. '*Inshallah*' – 'God willing' – was tacked on to any statement when the outcome was uncertain. '*Bokra*' meant 'tomorrow' and had the same careless connotation as '*mañana*' in the Latin world. '*Malesh*' – 'sorry' – was the half-apology offered to her whenever anything didn't meet her expectations. This allowed the other person to offer regret and save face at the same time.

April was now living in one of the largest nations in Africa, the Middle East or the whole world. Sadly, in spite of significant gold deposits and massive oil reserves, it had also become one of the world's poorest countries. Long years of civil war and military coups had tragically devastated both human and natural resources.

Religion was the crucial flashpoint behind much of the violence. Although Christianity pre-dated Islam, continuous invasions from Egypt and Arabia had left two-thirds of the land and people Muslim and Arabic-speakers. The remainder of the population were more obviously tribal and animistic, although they also reflected the influence of Christian missionaries and the West. Their determined resistance to Islamization was the main bone of contention.

Although April had no intention of getting involved in politics, she knew that she faced an uncertain future as she began her ministry. The capital was the crossroads for thousands of children who had lost their homes and families in the civil war, however, so this was where rescue work was most critical.

In actual fact, 50 million orphans were scattered across the continent of Africa, one-tenth of them in the country she had come to. A large proportion of these waifs were homeless because of war, separated from their families during attacks on their towns and villages. Fathers who were away fighting or who were killed often left their wives, mothers or aunts overwhelmed with the responsibility of feeding surviving children. As those children became malnourished, sick and ragged, they were forced to find work or beg. Although at first they might return home to sleep, they eventually lost contact with their troubled families. Other boys and girls ran away (or were driven away) after suffering neglect or abuse at home.

Diseases such as AIDS left many children orphaned, and destitution in camps for families internally displaced by war forced thousands of others to scavenge on the streets for their own food. Then there were the children who had managed to escape from slave labour or strict religious camps, and those who were born to girls or women who were themselves homeless or sex workers.

Over 10,000 boys and girls had found their way to the capital. These children represented many different backgrounds, tribes and ages. They seemed to be everywhere April looked.

27

It was impossible for her not to notice the boys who hung around the city's traffic intersections, ready to dash forward with rags to clean car windscreens before the lights changed. Some were so young that they could barely reach the windows. Other children staked out the exterior of fancy restaurants or banks to polish shoes or beg and to rummage through scraps of food thrown into the rubbish. The lucky ones turned up enough to feed younger siblings or temporarily fill their own hollow stomachs. Sometimes they fell into the hands of unscrupulous adults who trained them to beg, steal and make money for their masters. Most people regarded the urchins as little more than rubbish on the streets. They became invisible, living – and dying – unnoticed.

Perhaps 90 per cent of street children sought to dull their hunger pangs by smoking, drinking corn wine and sniffing a glue-like substance used to repair tyres. Solvent fumes stunned their brains and helped them, for a short time at least, to forget the dangers and hurtful memories that haunted their waking hours. It also lent them a false sense of bravado. If they should get caught picking pockets or shoplifting, the beatings wouldn't hurt quite so much.

Chemical highs left the children feeling dizzy or dazed and forgetful, and highly vulnerable to exploitation by predators who might expose them to sexually transmitted diseases. In return for their cooperation they earned a few pennies. If they resisted, they were beaten. Children who habitually used substances often suffered irreversible damage to the heart, liver, kidneys, lungs and brain, but such long-term consequences didn't matter much to those who struggled to survive from one day to the next.

The more April learned about the hopelessness of the city's rejects, the more they tore at her heart. She was told that hundreds sought refuge in *khors* – tunnels under the city that stored rainwater. Besides being dark, damp and unpleasant, such shelters were also hazardous. The tunnels could flood during the wet season; it was also not unheard of for the authorities to throw tear gas into the tunnels to smoke the children out. Sometimes they suffocated to death. Police also regularly collected boys from the street and put them in 'reform schools', which resembled young offenders prisons.

April spent part of each week as a special education teacher in an English-system international school. There she was responsible for creating and running a special needs unit. The students she and other teachers helped came from several different nationalities and were troubled by a variety of specific learning disabilities, adjustment or language difficulties. April often resorted to the internet for training and books about cases that came her way. She also trained other teaching staff, especially the learning assistants. Half the time she felt that she was keeping only one step ahead of the people she was instructing.

One of the children in her charge was seven years old and dyslexic, barely able to read. April and other staff members worked with this boy for a number of years, and he has now graduated from university and faithfully serves God. In fact, most of the children who received patient help at school went on to enjoy successful lives. They had simply needed to be understood.

April was overjoyed when Laura Jenkins, her friend and fellow teacher in Cairo, decided to join her at the international school in 2002. Laura had left Egypt after 11 years to care for her mother and further her studies back in the USA. Prior to her service in Egypt, however, she had actually worked briefly in the country where April now resided. So, when a teaching position came up at April's school, Laura was pleased to go there for two years and use her extra time to assist with the outreach to the street boys.

Unfortunately, in 2010, a new head at the international school decided to close down the special needs unit, neither understanding nor wanting such children in her school. April taught a shared class with Year 5 for another year, then transferred to Valley School, a private facility that employed Christian staff. This proved an even greater challenge than her previous post. Some of her students were born with Down's syndrome, one boy had autism and could not communicate, while another child had learning disabilities. Since she had not been trained to handle such conditions, April faced a steep learning curve, especially with the boy who had autism. Indeed, April was very grateful for the help of a colleague at the American school in the city who had a masters degree in special needs education.

What a joy it was to see the children make progress! During her years at Valley School, April learned to appreciate each small step, such as the day little Mohammed could sit and concentrate for 10 minutes instead of 30 seconds. When he was able to work alone and later responded verbally for the first time to something someone said, she was thrilled. It was frustrating that this milestone came just before she was forced to leave the country, so she never knew if he was able to maintain this progress.

Working at a large international school when she started her street kids project, April was exposed to the extremes of rich and poor. Her students owned so much in terms of material possessions, while the boys who came to the centre had so little. Teaching ensured that April had a visa to stay in the country, but at first it was very hard to deal with moving from one culture to another.

Early on, April began to attend an Evangelical church in the city near a large camel-trading market and a souk with endless side streets and alleys. She marvelled at the colourful kaleidoscope of clothing, food, household and hardware items on display. This market was also a favourite haunt of homeless children as there they could sometimes find discarded scraps of food or earn a few coins. This was one of the reasons April believed that God was leading her to open the first drop-in centre nearby. Knowing the church she went to had vacant property at the back of their building that might be used for this purpose, she prayed that He would plant that vision in their hearts.

Evangelical churches in the country were strong and very mission-orientated. The building where she attended church actually had services for four different language groups, besides the Episcopal Arabic Church. A great many congregations had been started by displaced Christians. Unlike believers in Egypt, they were not afraid of witnessing to Muslims, who were often nominal in their own faith. Churches were generally left alone in the capital at that time, although they suffered attacks in other parts of the country. Later the persecution became intense as Christians were no longer tolerated.

When April approached her church's pastor in October that first year to sound him out, she was delighted by his response. Pastor Elijah confided that the youth group had already expressed a desire to reach out to homeless children, but just didn't know how to go about it. The young men and women in the group were fairly mature, ranging in age from 19 to 30. After discussing the matter further, the pastor and council agreed that a patch of unused wasteland at the back of the large church property could be used for the project.

April began holding prayer sessions at the site with about 19 interested young people. Earnestly they sought God's guidance and, in November 1996, they began to clear away the piles of rubbish and debris on a 7- by 18-metre plot. They had no funds and no tools, so used their bare hands and a wheelbarrow April had bought with her own allowance. One side of the land was bordered by a broken wall about 1 metre high and a gate large enough for a truck to pass through. It was sweaty, dirty labour, but Jeffrey, Zack, Esther, Maxwell and most of the others who pitched in persevered, convinced that their project had divine approval. The joy of the Lord was their strength. Some of the boys at the SIM Centre were also eager to pitch in.

As they prepared the land, the team readied their hearts and minds for the ministry that lay ahead. Intensive prayer and Bible study were part of April's training sessions, which covered topics such as how to work with emotionally and behaviourally disturbed children. She brought in other people to demonstrate first aid. They all practised team-building and ways to work together, enthusiastically spreading the vision. In addition, the young people pursued their own research among kids on the streets and visited the SIM Centre and another German-run mission to see how they operated.

Other volunteers looked into the costs of employing builders, well-diggers and similar workers. An elder in the church named Atif was an engineer and a huge help in this area. Maxwell, a convert from the Coptic Church of Egyptian ancestry, also spent a lot of time and put a lot of effort into setting up the first centre through his contacts and skills. He and April spent days scouring second-hand markets, industrial dumps and other sites for cooking equipment, shipping containers for storing supplies and anything else that might prove useful.

Once, when they were out together in the market, Maxwell was highly amused when a man they had been talking to turned to him and remarked, 'You have a nice sister. Can I marry her?'

When visitors from Scotland arrived during this period, a mission leader asked April to drive them around the tourist sites. His wife chuckled. 'April knows her way to the well-diggers, builders, markets and metalworkers,' she told him. 'She has no idea where the tourist sites are!'

April was nevertheless given the job. Their guests wanted to see the boatbuilders first, and she felt sure that she could find the boatyard, since it was on the river.

'I have no sense of direction,' she admitted later, 'but I knew I had to go over a new bridge, because they had made the old bridge one way. I couldn't turn right after that bridge, however, and after driving round and round with those visitors, I couldn't find the river! I mean, seriously, I could not find the great river in the capital city? I was still driving along, giving my best tourist guide impression and sounding completely nuts.

'"Now, those are goats over there. We have a lot of goats wandering the streets – they are our rubbish collectors. Here you see a market. We have lots of open markets. Over there is a shack: these are very common, as people put up whatever shelter they can."

'Suddenly I stopped and, totally embarrassed, asked, "Does anyone know where the river is?"'

'Thanks to a Scot with a good sense of direction we found it. However, we managed to miss the boat builders. Remember, I was still quite new to the city! I searched the sand to my left for a boatyard (the river was on the right) until there was no more road. We turned round and then at last we found them: two half-built boats with a couple of guys working on them. This was the boatyard!'

Gradually the broken wall on the church property was repaired. As funds trickled in, April and her volunteers hired well-diggers to excavate a sewage pit. Next, they fenced their compound to create an open shelter kitchen where meals could be cooked. This area was located between the two shipping containers they had obtained and set at right angles in the corner of the plot. These containers could be locked securely overnight. One was used to store dry foods and cooking equipment, and the other eventually held the belongings of the boys who came to the centre, plus school supplies, toys, games and sports equipment.

Later, another metal and bamboo shelter was built, enclosed and divided into three classrooms. One open shelter had zinc roofing. When this structure half collapsed after a couple of years, staff from the international school replaced it and reinforced the roof with strong metal supports.

April had concluded very early on that their ministry would have to focus on boys. Boys far outnumbered girls on the streets, mainly because, during the war, girls were more often killed or abducted as slaves. Also as genders were strictly segregated in Muslim culture, offering one facility to both sexes was out of the question.

That first January, the team made sandwiches to take to the boys in the market and invited them to the compound on Friday afternoons. The children were happy to get a nutritious lunch and sometimes there were enough funds to serve a second meal during the day. The boys took the opportunity to wash their clothes and accepted counselling and a short spiritual challenge before playing soccer or watching a film. Since less than 20 per cent of children were educated, drop-in visitors also welcomed the chance to receive simple schooling in Arabic and maths.

Pastor Elijah remained a strong supporter of April's project through the years and ensured that boys who came to the centre were welcome to attend his church. A Christian doctor from the church also faithfully gave his time. Free treatment was an important contribution, because so many children suffered illnesses or abuse on the streets. Infections, fevers, cuts and bruises could be addressed by a team member certified in first aid, but some boys presented serious conditions, such as lost limbs, tuberculosis and epilepsy. One child required surgery for his crippled hand after it was held over a burning stick when he was younger.

Increasing numbers of boys showed up at the centre on Fridays as word spread about the good care they received, so Wednesday afternoons were added. After the official opening in April 1997, between 80 and 120 boys began dropping in on a daily basis. Ten of the young men and women who had been working at the centre part-time were asked to become full-time members of April's team.

At first, most of those on the team insisted that it was not possible to control their unruly visitors without physical force. Beating children with a stick or thick hose was the traditional way to enforce discipline in this culture. April disagreed and one day proved her point by running the whole afternoon programme for 50 teenagers without help – and without recourse to a stick! She taught the staff how to employ positive behaviour management and explained that some punishments – such as beating a child for every single infraction – would be as unjust as giving a thief the same sentence as a murderer. The boys themselves reinforced her point when they begged April to beat them rather than take their football away for a week. Most of the teachers saw that depriving the boys of their sport was far more effective than a beating that they were used to and would be over in a few moments. Even so, some of the teachers refused to change their methods and were asked to leave.

While the property was still being developed, boys and workers were forced to cope without proper bathrooms or running water. They had to use the church's overworked pit toilets and washed their clothes – and themselves – from a barrel. After many delays and frustration with the diggers, it was a great day when the compound finally got its own sewage system, complete with showers and toilets.

Even when they could only operate as a day centre, April could not resist taking in a few of the four- and five-year-olds and children who were ill, in need of 24-hour attention, to stay through the night. The youngest boy they ever sheltered at the centre was four and several were between four and seven. The team bought them straw sleeping mats that, while not ideal, were better and safer than the dirt floors of the public market.

Jeffrey, a member of the original church youth group who became a long-term staff member, remembered the first night that he, Zack and Maxwell slept on the mats alongside the children: 'We divided them into two groups, because we had bigger and smaller children. The teachers were in the middle. At midnight we woke up, because the boys were fighting, so we had to stop them, but slowly they became better behaved.'

As more supplies and help flowed in, the first rough drop-in facilities were gradually expanded to include a dormitory, bamboo classrooms and an office. They could now provide living accommodation for 50 boys aged 4 to 16 years. A further 25 or more children visited daily. April discovered that it was often difficult to determine a child's age. Even their mothers, when they could be located, were sometimes uncertain and could only link their son's birth to an event, such as a year of drought or unusually heavy rains.

Meals at the centre were simple but nourishing. *Ful* – brown beans baked for hours in a large pot – was the country's national dish and the main staple. Those who lived in the compound drank very sweet tea (milky tea for the little ones) and bread when they woke up, then ate *ful* for breakfast, supplemented with eggs, *tamiya* or salad if there was enough money. Lunch consisted of a one-vegetable broth, such as potato, *rigla* (green leaves) or sweet potato. This was made by first cooking onion and garlic in a lot of oil until it turned to mush, then adding tomato purée, seasoning and a bit of meat. After this had simmered for a very long time, the vegetable was added. This broth was served with bread and either a piece of fruit or salad. Supper consisted of lentil soup or aubergine salad – mostly the former. This menu plan allowed the boys to get their protein from lentils and beans, and vitamins from salad or fruit.

April grew very close to her local co-worker Esther, who partnered with her from the very first days in setting up the boys' centre. As April learned more of the young woman's history, she was moved. Esther had attended Bible school after finishing school and did administration for the church. Then, however, she had been taken advantage of by an older, married elder. She was stigmatized when she gave birth to a child.

Ever since she could remember, Esther had felt drawn to orphaned children. When she was going to college she passed through the market on a daily basis and started to befriend the kids she met who were living on the streets. She collected food from the college, offered it to them and built relationships. As the children opened up about their lives and how they lived, her passion to help them grew.

Esther learned that most boys had been drawn into a criminal network. One child could have three bosses: one man who was retired but knew the tricks, his younger deputy, plus a team leader. The older boss gave instructions to the middle man. The deputy trained the boys to steal and beg, and they turned in all their money to the older man, who gave a share to the others. The boys who brought in the most money won prestige, as well as a small cut in the proceeds. Those who displayed weakness and got caught and beaten by stall-holders or market visitors or chased by police might not receive any money. Every day new boys arrived from other areas and were drawn into the network and assigned to teams. Every day some boys died.

After college, Esther got involved with the church's ministries to women and children, until the day came when April approached the council about her project. This was the opportunity Esther had been waiting for. She loved the boys who came to the centre as though they were her own and became one of the most hardworking and faithful members of staff. Tirelessly she cooked, cleaned, stayed with any child who had to be hospitalized and did administration or whatever else was needed – even when there were no funds to pay so much as pocket money.

April was grateful for Esther's friendship as she struggled to establish the ministry. In the early days especially, April's identity tended to come from her work, so criticism of it seemed like a personal attack. It took years before she saw that her insecurities and desire to be accepted often led to her being oversensitive and defensive, making others perceive her as proud.

April remembers an occasion when she left a staff meeting in tears after being challenged, and withdrew to her office. A particular male staff member who was prone to being argumentative always seemed to be against her. April rarely cried; even as a child she had been rewarded many times at the hospital for not crying. Maintaining a British 'stiff upper lip' had served her well in times of crisis, but she also knew there was some pride involved. Esther loyally followed April to her office after the upset, anxious to reassure her.

Back in Egypt, counselling had helped April see the necessity of finding her identity in Christ. She knew that pride in any form was unacceptable for a leader and regular evaluations with a mentor helped her guard against blind spots. Nevertheless, she struggled for a long time with situations involving aggressive men, even if they were only verbally aggressive. It was some years before God brought her to the point of being able to deal with such men without falling apart. Every leadership committee she was part of in the country was composed of males, except for herself. So she started training her first team about friendship in relationships.

One day, one of the male students took her aside. 'You are too gentle and indirect,' he said. 'We can't follow that. If you want things to get done you must just tell us what to do. You must also be stronger with us. We are used to strong leaders.'

Later, April realized that she should have stayed true to herself by teaching the men to think for themselves and handle gentle leadership. Instead, she changed her methods and presented a tougher front. Because this strategy didn't stem from her natural personality, it became a source of stress and resulted, at times, in her becoming too forceful in her leadership.

> When I was younger I did not have a temper, but I developed one here. Partly this was due to working too long hours, and partly because of the type of leadership I had seen modelled. It was also a result of my attention deficit hyperactivity disorder and my insecurities. But whatever logical reasons I can give, in the end it was just sin. One Bible verse that challenged me was, 'human anger does not produce the righteousness that God desires' (James 1.20). I didn't lose my temper all the time, but it was there and a very bad way to handle staff. I feel I spent 17 years apologizing for this or that. One of the older team members, a pastor, said they had learned to apologize from me! I did later teach the team a non-verbal reasoning and logic method for handling things, because it was so lacking in their educational background. After this they were able to problem-solve, think critically and take the initiative much more.
>
> Personally, I am very analytical and like to investigate and question everything. This can be good for strategizing, but it is bad when it creates doubt or argumentativeness. It can also cause misunderstandings when people think you are against them and you are just trying to understand. In Africa, when a leader questions an idea, the subordinate doesn't enter into discussion but keeps quiet, believing they must submit. I have to train my teams to enter into discussion with me and express their opinions. Some of the older ones still won't do it, because it is so ingrained in them to keep quiet and do whatever the leader wants.

Although Esther was invaluable in making April aware of cultural errors she sometimes committed, culture clashes were inevitable.

Once, April asked the men on the staff why they were so lazy when it came to preparing meals, always expecting to be served rather than helping out. They looked surprised.

'We are not being lazy, Mama,' responded Zeb. 'In our culture men don't work in the kitchen.'

'You are learning to take care of children,' April pointed out, hoping to jolly them into a more cooperative attitude. 'If you also learn to cook, all the women will be chasing you to marry them!'

'No,' Jeffrey disagreed. 'If we learn to cook, our wives will be lazy.'

'What if your wife is sick? How will you eat?'

He looked at her in bewilderment, for in some tribes a man can always ask a woman to cook if he is hungry. 'A neighbour would prepare our food,' he assured her.

In the end, however, the shortage of female staff in the evenings meant that all the men in the team learned to put their pride aside and work in the kitchen. The boys also got used to cooking, cleaning and caring for their own clothes in addition to carrying out other practical chores in the compound. This was a big step.

It was the children themselves who came up with a name for the centre that first year.

'When I reached this place I found something was different,' observed one of the boys. 'I found many things I couldn't find on the streets, but the first thing I found here was the love. They treat us kindly! This is amazing for me, for the first time. Nobody cares about you on the street, but I found it here: the love.'

The boys all agreed that 'Love' would be a great name for the haven April had created for them. The 'Centre of Love' stuck.

4

Growing pains

———◆———

Speak up for those who cannot speak for themselves, for the rights
of all who are destitute . . . defend the rights of the poor and needy.
(Proverbs 31.8–9)

It was obvious from the start that simply caring for the physical and
material needs of the children who came to the centre wasn't enough.
This was only part of the solution, for the boys' emotional wounds
went very deep. Most had lost their families, all their possessions and
the place they had called home. They had also witnessed unimagin-
able horrors and suffered more in their short lifespans than anyone
should have to endure. Their aggressive behaviour reflected damaged minds and spirits that cried out for a healing the staff could not
give. Only the One who had created them, called them each by name
and sent His only Son to secure their redemption had that power.
The Father yearned for these children to become part of His family.
He waited with arms open wide, but He would never force them. It
was up to each boy to recognize that God's unconditional love was
for him and that nobody was beyond redemption. Coming to this
point sometimes took a long time. Meanwhile, team members did
their best to demonstrate the difference Jesus Christ made in their
own lives.

Street children were full of mistrust. They had often been
badly treated by adults, so they were slow to let down their guard.
Sometimes the boys told lies to protect themselves or to manipulate
other people. Or else they prevaricated to test someone, to see if he
or she was trustworthy. In order to survive they became experts at
deceit.

Sam arrived at the Centre of Love when he was around 15 years old. He had survived life on the streets for eight years, partly by join-ing a gang. Yet he was a quiet boy, hardworking and not naturally given to violence. He told the staff his name was Sam, that he was a Christian from the south and his parents were dead.

After the first year the centre ran into difficulties when one of the children fell ill and passed away. The church became more concerned with the need to have the ministry's paperwork in order and ruled that signed permission had to be obtained from existing relatives for children to live in. The staff urged Sam to try to remember the name of his town or village so they could perhaps locate a relative. He had previously insisted that he couldn't remember where he was from, but now he named a city in the south of the country. So one of the teachers who was from the same area took Sam on the nine-hour bus ride to find his family.

On the way, he said, 'Teacher Jeffrey, I have something to tell you. My mother was alive the last time I saw her, about eight years ago.'

'Why did you say she was dead?' asked Jeffrey.

'It doesn't matter,' Sam replied.

'Never mind. Let's hope that she is still alive.'

Further along the road Sam spoke again. 'I have something else to tell you.'

'Yes, son?'

'My name isn't Sam. My name is Mohammed. I'm a Muslim.'

When Jeffrey asked why he hadn't said so before, he answered, 'I thought you wouldn't take me because I'm a Muslim.'

'But son, we have other Muslim boys.'

'Yes,' Sam replied, 'but I was the first, and when I saw you accepted the others I was afraid to tell you I had lied in case you were angry.'

The teenager had said what he thought he needed to say in order to be accepted. It took even more time for him to fully trust his friends at the Centre of Love and tell them he had run away because the men in the village had beaten him and his father had not de-fended him.

Mohammed's mother was overjoyed that her boy was still alive. His father had died, but she told Jeffrey where his uncle lived, not too far from the centre in the capital city. She didn't want the boy to stay in a place where he could not go to school. Jeffrey took Mohammed to see his uncle, who said it was all right to keep him on the church property, but he had to attend the mosque with him on Fridays. When he was older he could choose for himself whether or not to attend.

The Centre of Love staff worked hard to locate the families or extended families of the boys, wherever they existed, and reunited them whenever possible. Of course, some children's origins were a mystery. One little boy, about seven, only knew his nickname, not his real name. People in the market where he was found said that he had appeared there when he was about three years' old and they didn't know where he'd come from. April was reminded of the song 'Nobody's Child', but this little boy had a heavenly Father who loved him and a new family at the centre who cared for him.

All too often the relatives the staff did manage to find were so impoverished or dysfunctional they could not contemplate another mouth to feed. Their homes, if they had them, were mud huts without electricity or water, and the little ones they still had with them were frequently malnourished and ill. One boy living at the centre had three younger brothers at home who were all in very poor health after suffering neglect by an alcoholic, mentally disturbed mother.

April had always been committed to working with relatives, and through counselling and micro-enterprise training see them brought to a level where they could support their families. Unfortunately, this dream didn't have time to come to fruition during her years in the country. When returning a boy to relatives wasn't feasible, the centre became his home, the other residents and teachers his family, until he was 19 – if he chose to live there. A few disabled boys remained into their adulthood, and later on a halfway house accommodated young men who needed a place to stay while learning to become independent or attending university.

'I used to live at home, but my dad died,' little Ramadan told staff.

My mum married again, but my new dad beat me all the time. My brother beat me, too. I kept running away and I got so fed up being beaten and nobody caring for me that I stole money from my stepdad and ran away to live on the streets.

When I was on the streets I searched for scraps to eat. Nobody cared for me. The police came and took me to a reform school. I hated it because of the way they treated us. We managed to escape one day. I kept looking for a job to try and survive. I discovered the centre and went there just to eat. Then they said I could stay. I am so happy there I don't want to run away again. I love to go to church and learn new songs. I love to play football. I am doing well at school. I hope that I can be a policeman, help children and help the poor. I would like to get married, too.

The youngest child they took in during those early days was Abel, whom April laughingly referred to as a four-year-old bundle of mischief. He later wrote of his childhood: 'My father was dead. Mum was always drunk and beating me, so when I was four I ran away. I used to eat leftovers in cafeterias. People were always beating us and taking us to prison. When I was five Jeffrey brought me to the centre. I was so happy to have a place to sleep instead of the ditch and to have food and school. Before I had no clothes, no one to care for me. I was dirty. Now I had people who loved me, I had food, clothes – everything.'

One of the teachers at the centre, Zeb, had found the grubby waif curled up in the market one day. The team eventually learned that his mother was a street worker who had been arrested and given a 20-year sentence for brewing alcohol. The market stallholders, who had a soft spot for the little boy, had been looking out for him.

Little Abel was never still. Always giggling and clowning around, he was happiest when he was climbing trees, rocks or walls. Part of his new life included going to church with April on Sundays. He sat beside her and managed all right through the singing, but the minute the sermon started he snuggled down and went to sleep. After a few months at the centre Abel climbed over the fence one night without the staff spotting him, and disappeared. It took many weeks of searching, but through police contacts Jeffrey discovered the little boy had been put into a children's prison many miles from the city. He went to see Abel and returned heartbroken.

'You would not keep an animal there,' Jeffrey exclaimed

indignantly. But only family could remove the child. By then Abel's mother had been found in prison, but she didn't know of any family members who would take Abel. In time, a non-government organization (NGO) that ran an orphanage visited the prison with Jeffrey and told the authorities, 'We are sorry. This is one of our boys; we didn't know where he was.'

After they had produced a letter signed by the mother, Abel was released to the care of the NGO. But he was a different child. Trauma and terror, beatings and abuse had broken the little boy's spirit. With a great deal of patience and love on the part of the staff he finally became more like himself, but Abel was never again the carefree clown of his earlier days.

By then April's drop-in shelter had developed into a live-in home. Abel asked if he could return. He remained at the Centre of Love until he was 14, when his mother was released from prison. Even after that he remained in contact; a quiet, loving boy who had learned that he could trust Jesus whatever else happened. Although Abel found it hard to adjust to a mother he didn't remember, he stayed with her and loved her. Eventually he finished vocational training school and got a good job as a builder. When peace came to the country, Abel and his mother returned to their home village, which he helped to rebuild.

Jarrell was another little boy the staff found on the streets, selling plastic bags in order to survive. He told them he had a brother, but didn't know where he was. Jarrell's mum had died and when his father remarried, the stepmother had treated the boys harshly before turning them out. This was not unusual behaviour; whenever a parent remarried, their new partner often rejected offspring from the previous marriage – especially boys. Girls could become servants or bring in money through their marriage dowry. The boys' father was a soldier and hadn't been around to intervene.

Jarrell settled in at the centre. He was not a lot of trouble, but occasionally he ran away, as others did from time to time. Even though the streets posed a constant threat, they missed the freedom of being without responsibilities or rules. As Andy Butcher explains in his book *Street Children* (1996), 'The street itself is an addiction stronger than any drug they use there. They need a lot more rehabilitation to get that out of their hearts and systems than the desire for drugs.'

On one occasion Jarrell returned on his own two days later – or so April and her co-workers thought. They scolded him for running away, but welcomed him back.

The child's response was puzzling. He insisted that he had never been at the centre before. That was when it dawned on everyone that Jarrell and his brother were identical twins! The whole time both boys stayed at the centre, April could never tell them apart. Apparently their stepmother was from a tribe that considered twin children cursed and demonic.[3] This was why the woman had whipped the boys severely and sent them away.

The staff were able to track down the twins' father and explain what had happened. He was relieved to find his sons. He said he knew they had been turned out on to the streets, and had been looking for them for three years. Arrangements were made for the twins to live with their father's brother and his family. They rebuilt their relationship with their dad, and were very content.

On the Christmas morning of her second year in the country, April attended church and was invited to lunch afterwards at a friend's house. When she arrived at her destination she discovered a very sick boy from the streets lying under a tree outside, covered with a blanket. Her friends told her they had found the child before church and given him food. However, his condition had worsened, so they gathered up the semi-conscious boy and took him to the hospital. On the way they stopped at the centre to pick up one of the teachers. The boy, whose name was Dennis, was about eight years old. After he was treated for malaria the doctor released him to the care of the centre.

'Dennis was our Christmas present,' April recalled fondly. 'He was very frail and stayed with us for quite a while. His parents had died in the war and his older brother was conscripted into the army, leaving him alone. When Jeffrey managed to contact the brother he was very happy to learn that Dennis was being looked after. After he finished his national service he asked the boy to live with him and the two were a comfort to each other.'

God blessed April with many close relationships in her adopted country. She even became 'auntie' to the children of one family she felt very much part of. For her health's sake – both spiritual and physical – she took six weeks off in the UK each year, longer on alternate years, to speak at churches and raise support for the project. Home visits gave her the opportunity to stock up on another year's supply of medications, and see her specialist. She also devoted time to her father. He still found it hard to live without his wife and told April that her company was the best medicine. They became very close. After internet access became more available to her, they connected every week.

Although she worked long hours and initially pushed others to do the same, April was also careful to set aside a 'Sabbath' day each week. She learned the hard way that always thinking she should be doing something 'more useful' with her time was wrong if she was refusing to enjoy the blessings the Father wanted to give her. Occasionally doing things just for fun or spending money on herself was not only acceptable but necessary. Since Sundays were too busy to be restful she allocated Fridays for prayer, reading and recreation. On the grounds of the third house she lived in was a big date palm tree; she liked to lay in its shade for most of the morning, interrupted only by Lady's occasional urgent demands to play.

Spending hours alone with God renewed April's spirit. But living in Africa meant that it was also important not to get so caught up in her ministry that she neglected the people around her. Forgetting to greet friends properly or focusing conversation on work, ignoring the concerns of others, was something she continually had to guard against. Being intentional about relationships meant scheduling one-on-one time with friends and making time for social events.

Occasionally she went camping in the desert with Swedish friends who had become her surrogate family, unfailing in their loving support whenever she felt the need. It was bliss to get out of the city with them and go for walks, sing together by a campfire and sleep out in the open. Such outings were restricted to two days, unfortunately, because their barrel of water only lasted that long. On other Fridays off April accompanied friends to a beach beside the river, a favourite place for many families and singles to mingle, picnic and cool off in the water.

The Centre of Love staff took the boys on a day trip to the beach once each year – twice when they could afford it. They put up a tent and charcoal burner so the children could feast, play football and splash in the river to their hearts' content. Of course, they also competed in making the most intricate sand sculptures, and enjoyed a rousing time of singing and worship before returning home. The excursion was one of their biggest treats of the year.

Another annual highlight was the Christmas party that was held at one of the centres the Friday before Christmas. Each child received a set of new clothes – shirt, trousers, shorts, socks and shoes – usually through a church in the UK. The boys loved to be nicely dressed and were very appreciative of this gift.

One year a new boy who had been out shopping for clothes with his teacher was returning on his own to the centre when he fainted, due to a low blood sugar level. The police picked Mathew up and, after accusing him of being drunk, beat him and put him into prison. A teacher took medical papers to the police to prove the boy was diabetic, not drunk. Although the authorities admitted they'd made a mistake, they wouldn't release Mathew until the next day, because it was Friday and their boss wasn't there. As a result, the boy missed the Christmas party and to top it off, someone had stolen his new clothes when he fainted. The disappointment was monumental to someone who had already lost so much in his short life.

If funds allowed, each child at the party was treated to a toy and sweets, purchased wholesale from the market. Usually a volunteer dressed up as Father Christmas or else April distributed the gifts to the boys and staff children. A local Korean church sometimes took part and they too generously contributed food and presents. Once the children received Operation Christmas Child shoeboxes packed with goodies, sent via Samaritan's Purse. The boys were thrilled to open the boxes, although some of the contents proved puzzling. One child tried to eat his tub of play dough!

The children also looked forward to entertaining their visiting friends and family with dramas and sketches, memory verses and worship songs they had practised. In the early years the young actors insisted on making a big deal of King Herod and his soldiers, and the murder of Israelite babies, in their nativity play. April guessed that this kind of violence had been made all too real to them during the war. Only later did the children focus on a more traditional nativity, as well as dramas that showed how God had changed their lives. The younger ones were always riveted by the testimonies of older boys who had once been like them, but were now so very different. The evening ended with the singing of Christmas carols led by the boys' choir. No one who attended could doubt they were celebrating the birth of Immanuel – the One whose name meant 'God is with us'.

The day after the party, boys who had relatives left to join them for a short time. Those whose family members were too far away took their holidays with some of the teachers who volunteered to host them.

The fact that many of the teachers on April's staff had lost their homes and come through harrowing circumstances allowed them to identify with the boys.

A former staff member named Ron shared:

I was around 12 years of age when I experienced war. I heard many different types of machine guns and saw people running and hiding. I saw people killed. Some died of hunger because there was starvation that year. The images of dead bodies and malnourished persons and small children disturb my memories even now.

My parents had a sharp dispute that caused them to separate temporarily. So my dad moved to the capital with me and four sisters, leaving my mom behind. But in the north my dad went off to another region and left us with his friend, whom he said was trustworthy. But this man was cruel to us. He beat me and the other children, so I started living on the street. When my mom heard about this she came all the way to collect me and rescue me. Sometime later she sent me to school.

I came to Christ when I was around 21 or 22 years of age, through reading a small booklet written by a man of God, Bill Bright. It was part of a series of booklets revealing spiritual truths. When I completed it I read the prayer that was written for anyone who wanted to accept Jesus as Lord and Saviour into their heart. I prayed that prayer, and it changed my life. God also used an Ethiopian evangelist, who explained more about Christ and helped me link up with the Fellowship of Christian University Students. I started growing spiritually and socially, too.

I first visited the Centre of Love through Zack, who was working there. Later, after praying to God for a job that could support me in my schooling, I went to the centre again and found out there were some vacancies for teachers. I first worked voluntarily for some time and then applied, was interviewed and accepted for a position.

In the beginning I only did my duties as a teacher and mentor, and filled my stomach with the food that was offered. Later I realized that the boys had their own needs. Some needed health care and others needed attention, because nobody loved them and they needed somebody to give them love. I tried to give what I could and spent a long time in the centre, leading many of the boys to the Lord. I believe many of them changed for ever. However, while I was mentoring the boys God was also working in me. I grew spiritually at the centre and God did great things in my life.

I am now working with an international organization as a child protection officer, and in the church I am serving with the young people and as an elder, assisting the senior pastor. However, I still have a zeal for street children and I will do that work in the nearest future, by God's grace.

By 1999 April had ten full-time people on her team and had appointed Benson, an internally displaced church member, to become director of the Centre of Love. She had actually wanted her friend Esther to take the position, but when she proposed this to the church committee they were horrified. A woman couldn't be leader, they stated adamantly. When April pointed out she was a woman, they said that was different. She was a foreigner! Years later the church changed its position and Esther did become the centre's first female director. Benson did not remain long and was replaced by Jeffrey, the committed young man who had been one of the youth group members at the church. Back then, although he had a part-time job, he helped to clear the property for the drop-in centre, and was wholeheartedly involved with reaching the street kids. He went on to serve in all the centres for the next dozen years until after his marriage, when he accepted a job as a translator for another ministry.

Two years after its official opening, the Centre of Love was not only full but bursting at the seams. In fact, the very smallest boys had to live alongside older teenagers, which everyone agreed was not a healthy situation for either age group. Most of the residents slept outside on mattresses at night, and dragged their beds into the church hall when it rained. Something had to be done to accommodate more children.

5

Equipped for life

But let all who take refuge in you be glad, let them ever
sing for joy. Spread your protection over them, that those
who love your name may rejoice in you.   (Psalm 5.11)

After praying long and hard about the situation, April and her
co-workers approached the Evangelical church to ask if it owned
another property that could be developed for the older street kids.
They were overjoyed to be offered a thousand square metres of fertile
farmland in an area about ten miles outside the capital. Adjoining
land was already being used for a Bible school, church and accommodation for pastors and students. Among the location's benefits
was its distance from the immediate temptations of city streets. It
also allowed space to grow food.

The older boys went to clear the undergrowth covering the plot.
After completing one section, Jeffrey – who had been director of
the first centre for the past year and a half – plus six of the teenagers
took their beds to the property and stayed there, sleeping in the
open air.

Jeffrey was chosen to oversee the building process and became
the first director of the new centre, while Esther took over in the city.
His first office was just two chairs under the trees. Later Jeffrey became April's deputy and then General Director over all the centres.
'Living on the new property was a challenge,' he related. 'The hospital
was far away and so was the market. The people in that area did not
want us. And the place had a lot of trees next to the compound, with
snakes and scorpions. But by the grace of God we eventually succeeded in having a school and a workshop to train boys from the streets to
have skills in car mechanics, carpentry and welding or metalwork.

We also took some of them to learn skills in a local vocational school. The best thing was that they accepted Jesus as Lord and Saviour, and some of them could preach and talk to people about Him.'

The new project to house boys aged 14 and older received impetus with a large donation, and an architect friend from the church designed the building plan. Workmen built a brick dormitory for 25 boys, followed later on by a second structure. Two residential staff lived in a smaller room located between the two dorms, with windows directed towards both of them. Bamboo classrooms, an office and kitchen, plus brick, long-drop toilets and showers were all slowly added to the compound.

The plan was to give the boys academic schooling in the mornings and vocational training in the afternoons, along with Bible and life-skills classes. Evenings were free for football, relaxing in front of the TV or engaging in youth group activities. Many of these young men would thus be equipped to return to their families as believers and wage earners, ready to give both spiritual and physical support. Two-thirds of the property was also cleared to grow vegetables, so boys could learn farming skills while helping with the feeding programme at both centres. This included planting some moringa trees, which had leaves noted for their nutritional value, and loofah plants useful for washing.

The new centre's first 25 residents were obviously delighted to exchange the dirt and danger of city streets for a home they could make their very own. Slowly they were able to grasp the fact that they were truly secure. No longer did they have to live rough, constantly looking over their shoulders and stealing or begging to fend off starvation. Now they knew where their next meal was coming from. Each boy became the proud possessor of his own bunk bed and locker. Once again April said a heartfelt *shukran* – thank you – for God's provision being above all that she could ask or imagine.

The reality of His protection was accentuated one night soon after the boys moved into the first dormitory. The phone jolted April awake at 2 a.m. with the heart-stopping news that the roof had collapsed on top of the children. The building had a roof constructed with bamboo beams and thatched with dried mud and straw mixed with concrete. A sudden deluge of rain accompanied by very strong winds had caused the roof to buckle under the weight of the wet mud. The winds had also created a vacuum under the roof, through the ventilation holes. Later, the team discovered that the builder had cheated them by substituting inadequate beams to support the weight of the roof. Added to that he had used watered-down, badly mixed concrete for the construction.

Before the rains had started that evening, fights had broken out between the boys, who were all relative newcomers from the streets. John, the teacher on duty, decided to separate them and put most of the teenagers into the four bamboo classrooms for the night. Only five were left in the dormitory. When the roof collapsed it fell in on one end, and was so heavy it bent the heavy metal bunk beds underneath. The roof beams, bricks from the wall and mud lay at an angle inside. At the top end of the beams' angle the bunks were untouched. All but one of the boys still in the dorm had been lying on these bunks. They were completely unharmed.

The other teenager was buried under mud for half an hour and his mates thought they would be digging out a lifeless body. Instead he was pulled from the wreckage without an injury! Had most of the boys not been sent to sleep in the classrooms, many would have suffered grievous harm or died. Also, if the other end of the roof had collapsed, the five remaining boys in the dorm would have been crushed. God had intervened to preserve those children's lives.

From the outset, both centres made it their aim to ensure a healthy balance of good food, medical care, recreation and education. The majority of the children had been deprived of the chance to learn to read and write. The second centre went a step further, equipping teenagers with training that would be useful for making a living. The school year officially started in July, and March and April signalled the end-of-year exam time. The staff prayed hard that all the boys would do well in their exams, especially those who were due to graduate. Some teenagers had to take Year 8 exams in order to go on to senior school. It was essential for them to earn respectable results in order to qualify for a further three years at a good school. The average age of graduates was 16, but young people from the centre were usually older, since they had started school later.

All the boys did a maximum of three years' schooling in the

centres; then they moved on to the church school. This was to get them out of their street habits and also prevent them from becoming institutionalized. Older boys who were in their major exam years also needed the more intensive interaction of a larger student body. Very young children started local school normally, without attending the centre. This meant the Centres of Love were obliged to come up with school fees for some of the students, as well as all of the school supplies. As time went on, partners inside the country, as well as Hong Kong, the USA, the UK and other places, generously came forward to sponsor promising senior school graduates so they could attend university.

Of course, the bamboo and mud school buildings inside the centre compounds also required extensive repairs every year. Brick schools would have been more durable, but it was difficult to raise the funds to build with bricks.

After examinations were over, the centres' schools – unlike mainstream schools – remained open. This gave an all-important structure to the days, helping to keep the boys from getting bored and also supplying extra tuition in areas they had struggled with in their exams. Additional classes were offered to expose children to a wider curriculum – subjects such as art, drama, crafts, practical science and music, which they didn't normally have access to.

During the summers the boys also enjoyed vacation Bible schools and, of course, plenty of sports and games. Those who had relatives could go to visit them for a month's break. This was intended to build relationships, although visits sometimes had to be curtailed because of family hardship or volatile situations. The staff visited younger children to ensure that they were not facing difficulties.

While most of the boys were away, the teachers took the opportunity to search for more 'lost treasure' in the market places, making initial contact with new children on the streets. This was followed by the difficult task of assessing each boy's situation and deciding which were most urgently in need of help. Sadly, there were always far more homeless children than they could accommodate.

Yet God's compassion often prompted His people to get involved. One time the headmistress of the international school, which had aided April numerous times, told her she knew an artist who was wanting to partner in a local project. April met with the lady, who then offered to schedule combined art sessions with kids from both the school and Centre of Love. The first one would be held at the centre and the next at the school. Both rich and poor children had a great time together just being kids, painting and using their creativity. The group decorated the boys' bunk beds and the backboard of the basketball nets, and brightened the compound with other fun projects.

During her visit the artist noticed that the centre's well was unfinished. When April explained the project had run out of money, the lady said that her boyfriend worked for a businessman and she would speak to him. This local Catholic man and his co-workers became great providers and friends of the ministry. Not only did they complete the well but they began to contribute to the running costs of the first centre. They even financed the education of two children belonging to widows on the staff, and collected toys and clothes from their church for the little ones. Eventually the group also supported boys who went on to university. God had clearly moved upon that businessman's heart and sent him to fulfil His purposes.

Local support even came from a Muslim businessman whose children attended the international school. He began sending free bread and cakes to the centres twice weekly from his bakery. April suspected the man baked a surplus on purpose! He also employed some of the boys in his factory when they were of age. Another Muslim contributed a sack of flour to the centre each month.

Assisting the doctor from the church was a Dutch lady physician; both of them gave free medical treatment and check-ups to the boys. The Swiss Mission Clinic also offered their facilities when it was necessary. A German nurse volunteered her time to care for a disabled boy who had become chronically ill. And a Christian lawyer helped the staff prepare legal papers gratis. The Lord's river of provision never dried up.

At one point April was forced to confide to prayer partners: 'One of my main problems at the moment is keeping my staff. I employ local people, but am unable to pay them a "living" wage; therefore I lose staff and the continuity of care which is needed.'

For three months April didn't have the funds to pay salaries.

Although she didn't understand at the time why God withheld this finance, the shortage served to prod several troublesome, uncommitted staff members to look for greener pastures. This resulted in a stronger work force at the centres.

Looking back over those years April affirmed that whenever she asked why, where, when or how, she was redirected to 'who': 'The one who calls you is faithful, and he will do it' (1 Thessalonians 5.24); 'And God is able to bless you abundantly, so that in all things at all times, having all that you need, you will abound in every good work' (2 Corinthians 9.8).

She unabashedly confessed:

I could not have stayed in Africa in my own strength. My physical limitations – the spinal arthritis and severe muscle spasms – meant that I lived with constant pain that hindered mobility. The spasms sometimes bent me to a 45-degree angle so that I was unable to move my legs. For a long spell I was mostly on crutches, and often unable to get out of bed. One of the team members who was like a brother to me made a table so I could do computer work from my bed, and I held many staff meetings from a lying down position.

In addition to the back problems I was diagnosed with malaria several times, although the testing methods in this North African country were not totally reliable in those days and any fever was called malaria. One time I was very sick because of a severe reaction to taking an anti-malarial medication. And like many others in that part of the world, I had to cope with frequent bouts of giardiasis – intestinal parasites – and infection from amoebas.

But I also wrestled with spiritual and emotional weaknesses, and these were often harder to deal with. Satan liked to remind me of my past failures in keeping a pure thought life, and used these memories to drag me down. I was afraid that God would give up on me, but He never did. It was many years before I realized that the fight was God's, and the victory was His already. He asked only for my total dependence and trust.

One dear friend who was a former teacher at my high school (also my mother's friend since the time they were teenagers) knew me well. 'I'm not surprised at what God is doing in North Africa. I'm just surprised He is doing it through you!' she admitted to me, with some humour. But she was not the first person to notice that the

Lord deliberately chooses the weak and foolish things of the world to shame the wise. From a human point of view, nobody would have chosen me to lead a team, serve in a difficult country and pioneer a new ministry. The fact that the Lord was able to accomplish all of this through one of the least of His children brought glory to His name.

It seemed to April that no sooner did she manage to scale one supersized hurdle than another loomed in her path. Fortunately, there were helping hands and hearts to pull her through each crisis, as long as she was humble enough to accept them. Often Spirit-led guidance, encouragement and rebuke came through the African believers around her. Her fellow workers in particular impressed her with the importance of committing all things, big or small, to the Father. He showed Himself faithful in responding to their simple, fervent petitions – and also the children's prayers – in astonishing ways.

Mark's case was a good example. Like many other boys who came to the drop-in centre, this 15-year-old was attracted by the free food, but he clearly held a grudge against the world. Mark lashed out verbally and physically at anyone who happened to be nearby. Everyone was afraid of him. But while the teenager enjoyed a sense of power through his aggressive stance, he was lonely on the inside. He didn't know how to relate to people normally. The team were at their wits' end in trying to deal with Mark; nothing seemed to get through to him. Finally, they met to discuss whether they should take the drastic measure of banning the boy from the centre, in order to protect the smaller children. They agreed to give him one more chance.

It was Easter time, so staff members had borrowed a television in order to show the *Jesus* film to the boys. Just as they were about to start the projector, however, there was a power cut. Everyone groaned. This typically meant a minimum outage of 12 hours. But one of the North African teachers stood up to suggest that they should all pray for the electricity to come back on.

April, who was at the back of the room, thought, *You can't pray that! It won't happen, and then what will the children think?* But the teacher led in a simple prayer to the Lord, and immediately the power came back on – another powerful lesson for the 'boss'.

The film touched Mark's heart deeply and by the end of the screening he was sobbing. Team members were a bit wary of approaching the boy, but one finally asked what was wrong.

'Jesus loves me,' Mark mumbled brokenly, tears still streaming down his face. 'Why didn't anybody tell me that before?'

Accepting that the Son of God had died for him, personally, broke the emotional dam inside Mark. Now that he had found a genuine source of love, he was able – even eager – to give it to others. April was astonished by the about-face in the teenager's attitude as she watched him over the next few weeks.

Eventually Mark was able to open up about the source of his deep hurt. He vividly recounted the day, years before, when soldiers had come to his village. He was eight years old, and all he could do was stand there, locked in helpless terror, while his mother was brutally seized and stabbed to death. His father was then hung from a tree. Sobbing, the traumatized child ran into the jungle.

For the next months and years Mark kept on the move, stealing food to survive and often being beaten for his behaviour. He had been put in prison three times, abused both physically and psychologically. Once he was free again he had hidden himself on top of a train to get to the capital city. There he lost himself among the throngs, figuring the only way to stay alive on the streets was to act tougher than anyone else.

Now, the teenager had discovered another option. The love he'd yearned for all those years had been demonstrated by the willing death of Jesus Christ on the cross; his place of refuge was now the arms of God. Mark stayed at the second Centre of Love for two years after that, and trained as a mechanic. Then he went to live with a relative. April was awestruck by the drama of Mark's redemption. It was the first time – but certainly not the last – that she witnessed God reaching into the heart of the most 'hopeless' of her boys.

Yet she herself had been the recipient of the Father's loving intervention on more than one occasion. Take the practical matter of transport. During her first two years she had relied on buses to get around the city. These were actually converted lorries, with benches lining both sides of the flatbed. The bus schedule was unreliable at best, and the bumpy journeys over rutted roads badly affected her spine. So during her third year she began driving an old car made available through gifts from her supporters.

One day while April was negotiating the busy streets, another vehicle abruptly pulled out of a side lane directly into her path. There was no possible way to avoid a collision, no time even to pray except for a lightning cry for help. Yet in the next second she found herself safely proceeding on the other side of the intruding car. She knew there could be no other explanation for her escape than the protective hand of God.

Shortly after the team had begun to construct the second Centre of Love, April was approached by a youth group from a church down in the south. This area had been devastated by years of attacks, leaving thousands of desperate, orphaned and uprooted children. These young Christians had seen the impact on street kids made by the church in the north, and were eager to extend the same kind of lifeline in their part of the country.

April had always dreamed of opening one shelter after another for this country's lost children, each of them functioning independently. Regretfully, she knew the resources just weren't currently at hand to help her visitors from the south. She urged them, however, to keep praying. As soon as it was within her power, she would act. In her October 1999 newsletter to prayer partners back home she shared the cry of her heart: 'We now have two homes and schools, accommodating a hundred boys, one with a vocational training school. Yet this is the tip of the iceberg! We need more homes and schools, and for this we need more workers and more funds.'

As usual, her all-knowing, all-powerful and ever-faithful God was already at work.

6

Lost and found

———◆———

But you, God, see the trouble of the afflicted; you consider
their grief and take it in hand. The victims commit
themselves to you; you are the helper of the fatherless.

(Psalm 10.14)

During the civil wars that ravaged many African countries, aid
workers witnessed a tidal wave of displaced and orphaned children pouring over the borders in search of a safe place to live. The
majority of these young refugees were male. Boys were more likely
to survive the long treks from bombed rural villages. Besides, girls
were often captured and exploited as sexual or domestic slaves by
invading soldiers.

Between 1983 and 2005, tens of thousands of boys hiked hundreds of brutal miles through the bush to reach the safety of refugee
camps in Ethiopia, Kenya and neighbouring countries after witnessing the torture and death of friends and families. The journey
often took months. Attacks by lions, hyenas, poisonous snakes, government troops and hostile tribes, starvation, thirst and exposure
claimed countless more victims along the way. Some children, overwhelmed by grief and terror, simply gave up. The boys who managed
to make it to the camps were often lost for ever to families, relatives,
homes and all that was familiar.

To April it seemed the years of civil war had acted as a huge
centrifugal force spinning children from their homes to lands they
had never seen. Hundreds of thousands more boys and girls were lost
within their own countries. For the fortunate few who had found
their way to the two Centres of Love that had been established, however, there was a chance for a new beginning. Even boys who no

59

longer had anyone to belong to could find a new identity and future as a much-loved part of God's family.

As April thought about the individual children they had rescued over the last few years, tears of thanksgiving filled her eyes. Many of the boys were unrecognizable from the desperate, hostile street urchins they had taken in. Each of them had bloomed in the caring atmosphere of the centres like flowers opening to the sun. The younger ones now behaved more like normal, fun-loving children anywhere. Most of the older boys had been set free from deadly addictions and negative attitudes, and were maturing into fine young men – proud sons of their heavenly Father.

Paul was one of those lost children. Until the age of seven he had led a carefree, happy childhood in a small village in the south, working on the family farm with his father and playing with siblings, cousins and friends. He had heard talk of war among the adults, but it all seemed far away and irrelevant – until the day government soldiers invaded his peaceful world. Shots and screams rang out as the men and women of his village were murdered and raped in front of his eyes, including his beloved parents. Others ran in panic, grabbing their children and trying to hide in the bush. Soon there were no adults left; they had either fled or were lying bleeding and lifeless.

The soldiers rounded up Paul and the rest of the sobbing, terrified children and trucked them to a distant location. There they were divided up. When one little girl kept crying, they shot her as an example to the rest.

Paul was taken to a farm many miles away where he was put to work as a slave. People in this country had been enslaved by invaders since ancient times, but in the 1980s the practice had been revived. Both pro-government militia and rebels were guilty of abducting civilians for forced labour, but during the civil war the government was involved in backing and arming numerous slave-taking militias as part of its strategy. In 2008 a member of the British parliament estimated that at least 35,000 men, women and children were still enslaved somewhere in the country.

Many of these slaves were Christians, kidnapped and forced to convert to Islam under threat of death. Sometimes their faces were branded before they were put to work as concubines, domestic help and farm labourers.

Unlike the farm where he grew up, the fields where Paul laboured seemed to stretch to the endless horizon. The clothes he had on when he was captured were soon reduced to filthy rags, and he was allowed little rest or food. The farm overseers seemed to enjoy beating Paul and the other children. One day the captives were shown a cross and warned, 'If you ever see a car or people with this cross, run – or they will catch you and eat you.'

Paul tried to run away from the farm, but he was soon recaptured. His captors took a knife and slashed him across his ribs to impress him with what would happen if he tried another escape. So great was his despair, however, Paul did make another attempt. This time when he was caught they nailed his feet to a plank. There was no more running.

One day foreigners came to the farm and informed Paul and some of the other slaves that they had arranged to free them. The strangers took him to a shelter in the capital city that held many displaced young people. Imagine Paul's joy and excitement when he discovered that some of the children were from his home village! The people in charge were kind and took good care of them, but one day they called everyone together to make an unhappy announcement.

'We're very sorry about this,' they told the young people, 'but we have no choice. We have no more money to keep this place open. We have to leave.'

So the lost children found themselves turned out on the streets, and took shelter in an abandoned building. One day when Paul was out trying to earn some money, he fell ill and collapsed. Some of the teenagers from April's centre found him and carried him home with them. The staff gave Paul the best care they could, but he was diagnosed with diabetes and needed professional help.

At first the boy was afraid to trust the Christians. Weren't these the people of the cross that he had been warned about? But eventually their patient kindness won him over. Paul took some of the centre's staff members to see his friends, and with assistance from the UN and Red Cross they found families or people from their tribe who would help them relocate back to their home areas.

Paul himself, along with another boy, stayed on at the centre because of his poor health, but he was content. He had found a family he didn't want to leave. Paul gave his life to the Lord and was so motivated to help others that he started to volunteer in another centre for street children.

April's team had been unable to locate any members of Paul's family, but one day the Red Cross informed them that the boy still had two living brothers. Paul went to meet them, full of excitement, but tragically one of the teenagers was shot by soldiers before he got there. The other boy disappeared, probably gone into hiding. Paul returned to the centre, but could not settle; he left again to search for his remaining brother. Sadly, although he was accompanied by a friend and carried sufficient food and medication, Paul collapsed and died on the journey. Although everyone at the centre grieved for the boy, they knew he had finally reached his forever home where there would be no more heartbreak. The heavenly Father Himself would wipe away all of Paul's tears.

Marial was born into one of Africa's tallest and largest tribes, whose 4.5 million people lived mostly as farmers and herders. During the civil war tens of thousands of these peace-loving residents were massacred by government troops, with left-over orphans crowded into refugee camps.

Marial had fled to the capital city with his mother years before. When he first began turning up at the centre, he was moody and uncommunicative. Not all the boys chose to live in, because they didn't trust anyone, but Marial kept returning until eventually he decided to stay. After a while he felt safe enough to reveal that he had run away from his mother after she stabbed him with a knife. The team still felt they should contact the woman, but when she finally presented herself at the centre she declared that she didn't want anything to do with the 13-year-old.

'I hate him,' she told the team flatly, only adding without explanation, 'He is very bad!'

Marial was shattered by this denunciation, but over the next four years God had brought healing. The boy's heart had been deeply touched through a film they'd shown at the centre called *The Prodigal Son*. He was now 17 and a very kind, happy and helpful young person, close to the Lord and sensitive to others' feelings. At one point Marial tried to live at home again with his mother, but he could not cope with her hostility. So he had returned to the centre after three months. He hoped, one day, to become a minister and share the message of Christ with other people who needed to hear His good news.

Lester was another boy who had known hunger, thirst and abuse on city streets since he was a small boy. By the age of 17 he had built a hard and bitter shell around his vulnerable inner self. It seemed impossible that his abusive attitude would ever soften, although he had been dropping in at the centre, on and off, for three years. The staff could not seem to get through to him.

Then, in May of the previous year, the second centre held a one-month Bible school for the boys. Lester was deeply touched by what he heard. From that time on they had seen the same near-miraculous change in his outlook that they had witnessed so many times before in other boys. Lester was delivered from his addictions and matured into a well-mannered, hardworking young man who loved Jesus Christ as his Saviour and best friend.

April could name a hundred instances of God's merciful intervention over the past years. The boys could rely on sufficient food to eat and were growing strong in mind and body. Medical treatment, combined with intensive prayer and spiritual nourishment by the Centre of Love family, made healing possible for even some of the most seriously ill and injured.

Fourteen-year-old John, in particular, sprang to mind. Shortly after finding a home with them, the boy was diagnosed with a severe case of meningitis. The team watched helplessly as his body was racked by more than 40 grand mal seizures within two days, before he fell into a deep coma. They arranged for specialists to visit the hospital and assess John's condition. All of them agreed the boy's brain was so badly damaged that death would be a kindness. If he lived, they said, he would be as helpless as a newborn baby, unable to care for himself.

Everyone at the centre prayed all that night for John. The next day April drove back to the hospital. When she walked into the ward she stopped in her tracks, stunned. The boy was sitting up in bed!

'Good morning, Mama!' he called out cheerfully. April continued to stare at John in disbelief. God had obviously heard their prayers and reached out to heal a condition the doctors had written off as hopeless. John suffered no after effects from his illness and was released from hospital strong and well.

Abdu had shown up at the compound two years before. The 15-year-old had run away from his home hundreds of miles distant, when he was eight. He had managed to scrape along for seven years by selling plastic bags on the streets. He trusted no one; glue and corn wine were his only comforts. At the centre he was very withdrawn except for occasional outbursts of anger. Then the Lord softened his heart through the friendship of one staff member in particular.

With a lot of patient help and prayer Abdu was able to overcome his addictions. He also learned to read and write, and was training as a mechanic at the older boys' centre, receiving very positive reports from his teachers. The teenager still refused contact with any member of his family. If they were still alive, he said, they would be very far away in the south.

Tombe was 13 years old. He and his uncle had fled from the fighting in their home village and they lived in a displaced people's settlement until his uncle could no longer feed him. For the next year the boy depended on finding scraps in the public market, until getting help at the Centre of Love.

Tombe had been very aggressive at the start, but as he learned that he could trust God to care for him he was able to give up sniffing glue. Within a few years he had developed a much happier outlook and was making great progress at school. One of the teachers had gone with him to try to locate his uncle, but they were unable to find any trace of the man.

Ernest was another 13-year-old who had suffered neglect after his mother's death. After running away to the capital he lived in the market area for five years, living hand-to-mouth before hearing he could get free food at the drop-in centre.

Glue addiction had made Ernest very combative; he was a tough boy to handle and caused the staff no end of problems – until the Lord broke through. Since then there had been a wonderful revolution in Ernest's behaviour. No longer dependent on chemicals to anaesthetize his brain to stop the nightmares that haunted him, the young man had become calm, cooperative and hopeful of making something of his life.

Lennie, aged 14, did not want to talk about why he had left home. The streets had been all he'd known since he was small and he had become entangled in many forms of substance abuse. The young man's behaviour at the centre was initially very disturbed; his uncontrollable anger erupted in fights and he ran away many times. The other boys nicknamed him 'thorn boy'. But after living there for some time and attending school, the Father eased his hurting heart. Lennie was gradually released from the addictions that weighed him down and his behaviour rapidly improved. The teenager's new goal was to become an evangelist and tell others how their lives could be transformed by Jesus, as his own had.

Andrew was 13 years old when he met up with April and the team. He had been born in the mountains, a green and beautiful area that was home to about 50 tribes, each with its own language and particular Christian, Muslim or traditional religion.

Unfortunately, this territory was one of the hotspots in the civil war. Arab raiders kept intruding to confiscate land and cattle, while soldiers looted and burned villages, carrying children off into slavery. Later on, a ceasefire supposedly granted autonomy to the region, but bombing continued almost daily. Tens of thousands of residents fled over the borders to neighbouring countries, seeking refuge.

When Andrew's father died, his mother had no way to take care of him. The boy walked and hitched rides all the way to the capital city; there he lived off rotted and discarded food in the market for two years, before finding his way to the centre. Andrew was not a difficult child and settled in quickly. He visited his mother regularly, but could not stay with her as she was still unable to feed him. He put his faith in Jesus, and it showed in his cheerful disposition.

Another boy from the same tribe, 12-year-old Abdel, ran away from home. Somehow he survived the streets for two years before finding refuge at the Centre of Love. It took a long time for him to confide the truth about his origins, but after he was patiently weaned from his cravings for drugs he settled down. His mother and father were happy when the centre sent news of their son. They took him back home so they could raise him in their faith, and he readjusted well.

Eleven-year-old AJ's father had many wives and neglected the child and his mother, who apparently suffered severe mental problems. AJ ran away from her when she could not feed him or care for him adequately. The staff didn't know how long he had subsisted on the streets before they took him in and made contact with his mother and father separately.

The woman said she wanted to take AJ home and raise him in the tribal culture, but the father travelled to the city to explain that she was mentally unfit to care for the boy. Since he was unable to do this himself, he wanted his son to be raised at the centre. AJ made it clear he didn't want to go home; in fact, he became agitated if anyone even broached the idea. So he stayed on, grew to love the Lord and particularly enjoyed opportunities to sing in the church's junior choir.

Sol was another runaway, fleeing a violently abusive father after reaching his teens. After trekking many long, hot miles he ended up in the country's largest city where, like so many others before him, he begged or stole or picked up whatever food he could find to stay alive. Sol started living at the second centre when he was about 15 and proved eager to please and was uncomplaining. After two and a half years he started training as a mechanic, returning to the centre to attend night school. Sol visited his family only once, because they were so far away, but they expressed satisfaction that he was safe and learning a vocation.

Nobody knew where 13-year-old Benny came from. This boy had tragically lost both of his legs from mid-thigh down when he was just seven, after sleeping on top of a train and rolling off under the wheels. The year following this accident his mother and sister died. The child lived a short time with his father, but the man deserted him, so Benny was left on his own to beg on the streets. By the time someone finally brought him to the Centre of Love he was in a bad way. The team took Benny to a Dutch hospital and convalescent home to be fitted with artificial legs. Once he was ready he went to live with an uncle they had traced.

Remembering each of the lost boys who had been found and transformed in body and spirit, April's heart was full. So often she found it hard to communicate to others the wonder she felt at seeing the beaming smile of a healthy child replacing the sad visage of one who had come to them sick and suffering. How could she convey what it meant to see young Lester, for instance, gently caring for a toddler in church and realizing what a fine, gentle boy he had become? The former sullen, disturbed teenager had entirely vanished.

Whenever she felt overwhelmed with problems, April went to spend time with her boys. How could she stay discouraged when she looked into their faces? It was impossible to express her emotion when Marial led worship or Tombe shared from the Bible on a Sunday morning, so full of confidence and conviction. What mature young men of Christ had replaced the violent, abusive young addicts who had come to their centre! Then there was Ernest, praying from his heart in church and thanking God for all He had done. Was this really the boy no one could control? Only God could work such miracles in children who had been uprooted and abused or forgotten by society. They had learned to play and dream again, as children should, of one day having their own families and becoming teachers or doctors or pilots.

Perhaps, she thought, parents who had observed the subtle changes in their own beloved children as they matured could understand. The countless precious, quiet turning points in her adopted sons could never be recorded on paper; only etched on the heart. But this April knew: the value of even one child's life was beyond price. She could not praise God enough for all He had done. Nor could she ever give adequate thanks to the hundreds who served as willing partners in the work. Her friend Laura had stayed for three years before needing to return home to care for her mother in the USA. Others too had selflessly come to this North African country to lend their efforts over short or longer periods. Scores more had prayed and sent regular support, committing themselves to children they would never meet.

For April such commitment was easy, for she could see the daily evidence of God the Father at work in her boys. Partners overseas could only use their imagination. Perhaps they didn't really grasp the reality of the miracles they were enabling through their faithfulness. But one day, in eternity, they would meet the living evidence face to face.

7

Spreading south

————◆————

So do not worry, saying, 'What shall we eat?' or 'What shall we drink?' or 'What shall we wear?' For the pagans run after all these things, and your heavenly Father knows that you need them.

(Matthew 6.31–32)

Two years had passed since opening the second Centre of Love for older boys. God had prospered the work. In fact, not only did both centres have sufficient funds to cover staff and operating costs, they actually enjoyed a surplus! April and her team were certain this situation hadn't come about by chance, and asked the Lord what He meant them to do.

Almost simultaneously they were visited by a believer named Samuel from the same church group that had approached them earlier, from the south of the country. Samuel had the same passion to help street boys in his area and was determined not to go back empty handed. He presented his vision to the Centres of Love and to another international mission in the capital, hoping for support. April's team joined Mission 21's staff in seeking God's will, and agreed to share responsibility in setting up the new ministry in 2002. This turned out to be the third Centre of Love.

April felt frustrated when her ongoing back problems kept her from overseeing the development of this project in person. A ten-hour drive on unpaved roads was beyond her, however, so she nominated Jeffrey to go instead. He had been with her from the start and she trusted him implicitly to help Samuel supervise the construction and organization of the new centre. A few years later, on the very day a paved road finally reached this town, Director and Founder Samuel phoned April and happily announced, 'Mama, now you can come [visit]!'

After encountering long delays and opposition in getting building permission at their first choice of property, the team decided to use a smaller plot of land that already had permission to erect permanent buildings. This would also put them closer to the market, saving transportation costs.

When April eventually travelled to the new facility, the town was so undeveloped she could walk from one end of it to the other. The land purchased for the new boys' centre was very inexpensive at the time, situated on a side of the road where there were few other buildings. The property appreciated in value as more and more shops sprang up, but initially electricity was only available once a day. Kindly neighbours allowed the boys to use their power until the civil war drove them into refugee camps. A second piece of land was planted for farming.

Samuel fully embraced the ministry and became a true father to the 40 or more boys in his charge. He ran a loving and efficient programme that covered the children's physical, educational, spiritual and counselling needs, and they enjoyed a real family atmosphere. Plants and flowers growing on the compound added a pleasant touch. So did the chickens that were allowed to roam free. The boys at the centre ranged in age from 4 to 18 years old and they helped to sustain themselves by growing some of their own food and catching fish in the nearby river. Later a vocational programme was started in conjunction with local people, who took on older boys as apprentices. In addition, Samuel and his dedicated team worked with families in the community and partnered with the children in doing evangelistic outreaches. They even held a programme at a prison each month. The young inmates looked forward to their visits.

Of course, Samuel could not protect his boys from all the hazards that came with living in the south. Diseases such as typhoid, meningitis, cholera and malaria were commonplace. Cerebral malaria claimed 12-year-old Joseph after he had lived at the Centre of Love for two years. Joseph had run away from home because his father, mentally unstable after serving as a soldier, beat the boy and chained him up. His mother had found him in the streets one day and taken him to the centre, where he had been very happy. Everyone grieved Joseph's passing. Seven other children and the director also fell ill with malaria, but fortunately it was not the same deadly strain.

Samuel and his staff regularly arranged for the boys to visit their families, where they existed, but it often proved difficult to re-unite them permanently. Many families were destitute. Parents also needed counselling, which the centre did not have the resources to supply. Sons sent back to such troubled circumstances were at risk of abuse, malnutrition and disease; more than likely they would also have to give up any chance of an education and return to working or begging on the streets. Yet family links were important and staff members did their best to maintain them.

One of the residents at the new centre had actually lived previously with his family in the north of the country. Fed up with being beaten by his father, Adam ran away from home and lived most of the time in the market. April was shocked by a picture the child had drawn, showing how his father bound and beat him on the rooftop of their house.

Adam explained that he had learned how to steal things in the market to survive, but, he added, his father still found him and abused him. Then his grandmother died down in the south, and Adam's family took him along for the funeral. He related:

> After the funeral I ran away to live on the streets because I didn't want to go back with them. I used to swim in the river and eat scraps from the café. I used to fight, too. I was addicted to corn wine that they made on the streets. I found teacher Samuel in the market and then my brother found me and got my mum. She took me home, then decided to take me to Samuel at the centre so that I would be safe.
>
> I have many good friends in the centre. I go to the school and learn many things and I have reformed now. We play football. We also have devotions every day. And we have good food. When I grow up I want to be a great architect. I will have a happy wedding day and I will have a happy family.

April thoroughly enjoyed her visit to their third Centre of Love, staying in a traditional mud hut with a grass roof inside the church guest compound.

'We were warmly welcomed by the people,' she recalled. 'After church the female elders honoured us by washing our feet and hands, and making us a huge breakfast of fish and local foods.'

April and her companions had brought small gifts for the boys and held a special Bible programme for them. They also ran a short course for the teachers from the centre, inviting other local teachers as well.

When darkness fell at seven o'clock only sporadic electricity was available. April went to bed early, knowing the pre-dawn wake-up call from the neighbourhood's roosters would quash any possibility of sleeping in. The cockerels' chorus triggered the loud barking of dogs and this, in turn, spurred the braying of local donkeys. No alarm clock was necessary. For April, never a fan of city life, it was all a delight. She was in love with the programme, the people and the simplicity of this part of the country, despite its many problems. She and her companions even enjoyed the long car journey back to the capital, which took them through innumerable small towns and villages with beautiful flowers, fields and varieties of cattle, goats and camels. They also admired the trees and shrubs that grew along the banks of the great river.

Some years later Samuel made April's father an honorary chief of his tribe and presented April with the chief's stick, necklace, wrap and bracelet to take to him, since he was not well enough to travel. Children were also named after him, although there was some confusion, because tradition dictated that a person's second name was their father's first name. April was touched when Samuel told her that because her father had allowed his daughter to continue with her mission in Africa rather than staying at home in England to take care of him after her mother died, he wished to honour her family.

Samuel also named his first daughter April. She would always feel humbled that he had remembered her family in such a way. To her, the commitment of this man of God far outweighed anything she had done.

Esther, the young woman who had worked alongside April to pioneer the first Centre of Love, conferred a similar honour. When James, who had succeeded Jeffrey as the overall manager of the centres, moved away, Esther took over and remained leader at the time when Christian ministries in the capital came under fire. She was also a senior leader in her denomination's women's ministry. By now she was married and had three children. When she fell pregnant again in her forties she expressed regret, because she was already struggling to provide for her family's needs.

'Never mind,' April comforted. 'This one is a gift from God; He will provide.'

The new 'one' turned out to be twins. When April arrived at the hospital following the births, she learned that Esther had named one infant Jody and the other John, after April's father. Esther explained that because April was serving in a mission she didn't have a chance to marry; therefore, her father had no grandson to name after himself.

April was touched, and never corrected her friend. When the twins were five years old Esther's family made a special wooden plaque, painted by the boys, to send to April's father in England. He was very pleased, and made sure little John's photo always held a place of honour on the mantelshelf.

8

The quality of mercy

But if anyone has the world's goods and sees his brother in need, yet closes his heart against him, how does God's love abide in him?

(1 John 3.17, ESV)

Tragic decades of religious conflict in April's adoptive country gradually created one of the highest populations of internally displaced persons (IDPs) in the world. By 2006 the number of men, women and children who had become refugees within their own land, through no fault of their own, topped five million. The majority of these homeless people resided in IDP or squatter camps on the fringes of the capital.

Government-assigned settlements for displaced men, women and children were located in the desert, a considerable distance from the city centre. This meant most people found it difficult to get jobs that would earn enough even to cover daily transportation costs. Nor was it possible for them to grow their own food in the arid desert soil.

Non-government organizations (NGOs) from around the world responded to the urgent plight of these desperate millions, working with national staff to provide shelter, food, medical help and other basic needs. Some Christian groups even helped local churches organize schools for displaced children. These schools included a daily breakfast for students and became instrumental in keeping several thousand children off the streets. As one worker expressed it, 'Education is our future. If our children are educated and also instructed in our faith, then we can rebuild our country in peace time.'

Teachers who worked in the camps were often displaced themselves. April knew believers like this man below, who had his own harrowing story.

I lost my parents when I was a child and was raised by my uncle. I was able to finish my primary education in our town in the south, but then the problems there became so great due to the war that my uncle was no longer able to pay school fees. His son left school, and so did I. I cleaned shoes and fished, trying to provide for our needs. However, it became too dangerous to live in our town, so we ran away to the capital city.

On the way our bus was part of a convoy of buses, but the driver broke his leg so we had to separate. As each bus travelled along alone, the nomadic people in the bushes stopped many of them. They tortured and killed all the southern people that they found. By God's grace we arrived at a town unharmed. It was our intention to ride on top of a train for the rest of the journey, but we discovered that the week before, 600 passengers from the south had been burned in the train. So we decided to walk.

In all it took me 25 days to get to the city. From there I continued my journey to try to find my younger uncle. When I found him, he told me it was too heavy a responsibility for him to take care of me. So I found myself alone again, and I decided to return to the capital. I worked day and night as a baker until I could save enough money to continue my schooling. Because I had no documents to prove that I had been in school I had to take an exam, which I passed. I studied and worked to pay for my schooling, and because of this I failed my final exams twice, but the third time I passed. I was then accepted into the university. Now I am a teacher in one of the schools for displaced children.

After over a dozen years of dependence on overseas donors, local churches took over the responsibility for supporting national teachers in the camps. Eventually they also provided the children's breakfasts and school supplies. This was an important step towards local sustainability.

At one point, the government ordered the demolition of thousands of refugee shelters in the IDP camps. Their idea was to sell plots of land back to those who could afford it; unfortunately, for most this was out of the question. Many families lost their property and were left without protection from the elements. NGOs did what they could to deal with the emergency, raising funds for vitamin-enriched milk powder to strengthen children aged one to three years old who had started to show signs of malnourishment and weakness.

They also distributed mosquito 'tents' to ward off malaria, and locally made blankets specially designed as body wraps for cold desert nights. Later on, micro-enterprise projects were set up in the camps.

While continuing to direct the street children's project and teaching special needs children part time, April was glad to help such efforts wherever she could. For a number of years she did administration work for one of the NGOs and supervised a local Egyptian Coptic Christian from an Evangelical church who took care of the bookkeeping. Preparing reports in English for prayer and financial partners was another essential contribution. Later, when she was forced to hand over the administrative work and leave the country, April regretted her lack of foresight in not ensuring that more national staff took language classes.

When the Iraqi war erupted in March 2003, several parts of North Africa reacted angrily to the invasion of Iraq by a United States-led coalition. People on the streets started attacking foreigners who looked like Americans. April was on her way home from work one day when her car got caught in a mob of about 200 angry students wielding sticks and throwing stones. The protestors were closing in on her vehicle; their intentions all too clear, when she spotted a man from a nearby fried chicken restaurant gesturing urgently for her to drive into his compound. Without hesitation she turned the car. It was difficult to make any progress, since the mob surged around three sides. The back window was smashed. But standing protectively in front of the vehicle and by the two front passenger windows were four very large men with their backs to April. The crowd was unable to get to her. Once she'd reached the safety of the compound unharmed, she glanced at her rear-view mirror. The manager and four men were closing the gates behind her.

The next day, with April and all foreigners ordered to remain indoors, friends took a gift of sweets to the restaurant to thank the five men for helping her. The manager's face registered surprise. 'I was alone!' he told them.

April was awestruck, realizing that God had once again intervened and sent His angels to protect her. How else could one man or even five shut the gates in the face of over 200 angry rioters?

In 2004, the decision was made to move the younger live-in boys to the second Centre of Love for a time. This allowed staff to re-instate the first centre's drop-in ministry and reach out to more boys on the streets. It also allowed April to minimize the number of full-time staff and reduce expenditure during a period when finances were tight. The first centre could mostly be run by volunteers.

The transition went very smoothly. The total of 52 boys ranged in age from 7 to 19, and they soon got used to living together as one large family. April hoped that by January of the following year they could take in some of the youngest drop-ins and raise the number of residents to 80.

That same year a new programme was launched to support the centre's graduates who were still living in the capital city. These boys were invited to a weekly get-together and Bible study. An evangel-ist worked full time to help them find jobs, visit them at home and follow up with their schooling.

Residents could stay at the centres until they were 19, although many chose to return to their families or relatives before that. The vocational training they received not only helped them gain confi-dence in new skills but generated much-needed income. Products made by the teenagers sold well in special bazaars held for the public. Profits were divided to allow the boys some pocket money, and they were also given a voice in how the balance was to be spent to benefit the centre. Among their creations were miniature donkey carts and tuk-tuks (motorized rickshaws) crafted from wire and scrap, and other wire ornaments such as lizards and crosses. From wire and bottle caps they made items such as tortoises and snakes; metal candle holders of different designs and plant pot holders were also popular. Some boys built furniture out of both metal and wood, and orders were happily taken by the carpentry shop to produce more such items for foreigners and church members. In addition, those who had an aptitude for art sold their paintings and teen-agers who took the mechanics course repaired cars and bought scrap vehicles to rebuild and sell at a profit. Even the alfalfa grown on the property could be sold for donkey fodder. April was proud of the boys' initiative.

Part of the project's success in later years was due to volunteers like 24-year-old American Brenna Atkins, who had felt God calling her to experience working with orphans and other vulnerable children in Africa. A contact put her in touch with April, and she invited her to join them. Brenna gives us insight as to what life was like at the centres.

Living in this particular North African country was not what I'd had in mind, but it was the door that opened and I moved there, sight unseen, in 2011. With April's blessing I slowly learned Arabic and started teaching the boys at both centres a bit of art, then also handcraft techniques. They caught on quickly and soon they were making all manner of interesting sculptures and pieces using wire, bottle tops, and other repurposed (and thoroughly cleaned!) garbage. We were able to start generating income for the centre and the boys, and April was always available to answer questions and offer insight and encouragement. At the same time she gave me a lot of free rein to use my gifts for the hopeful benefit of the boys' lives.

Let me tell you, I loved those former street boys. The younger ones especially, but all of them really. I loved playing with them, painting with them, teaching them to draw, trying to talk with them, sharing my headphones, giving them my camera.

It wasn't all cupcakes and roses, of course. Sometimes the kids ran away or stole. Got into fights. Beat each other. They could be incredibly whiny and selfish. They usually moaned when it was time for art, even though I know for a fact that most of them really liked it. They didn't ever say thank you in words. But there were beautiful moments of grace and love that I saw each day, like one of the older boys taking time to joke around and play with a younger one. Offering me cool water to drink instead of my warm water bottle. Cheering for each other in the group soccer game. Giving another child the last bite of their food. Taking care of one of the boys, who had broken his foot, without being asked and without conversation or comment, just picking him up and moving him to where everyone else was going. Taking paintbrushes from my hand and washing them out for me. One day I took my shoes off to play soccer and a boy took his flipflops off and offered them to me because the field had stones and thorns.

Usually the boys patiently repeated their Arabic so I could figure out what they were saying. They laughed when I shrugged my shoulders in resignation because I really had no idea. They would ask about the next time we would be painting or drawing, and when I walked through the gate at least one boy called my name and smiled, which oh, so warmed my heart. They would enthusiastically ask me if I was going to play soccer with them that night. Certain ones loved to sit with me to learn to draw things or to show me how to write Arabic words. They made me laugh.

Most of the boys at the centre had been addicted to glue and other drugs when they first came. They had all been through serious trauma, their families all broken in some way. The staff were amazing, but they were mostly men, which was good and appropriate for that situation. But it did mean that the boys weren't being parented in a traditional sense. So I wanted to do what I could for those whose mothers, for whatever reason, couldn't mother them. Be a surrogate big sister, a teacher, a friend. Use the gift of art for therapy, connecting, and hopefully enrich their lives somehow. I wanted to help them grow into godly men: to see truth, feel loved and be well cared for.

This was my perfect place and I absolutely loved it. I was looking to expand what we were doing when a mass expulsion hit many Christian organizations in the area. By May 2013 everyone I knew was out or arrested. I was expelled with all of the other foreigners after only two years in the place that, with the help of April Holden, I'd loved and made my home.

I moved across the border with hopes of being able to go back at some point and work again with the boys. I was devastated to leave them and wanted desperately to go back, though that is a door that has been decidedly shut and isn't safe for any of us to re-enter at present. For the next year and a half, on and off, I lived and worked at a street girls' centre, using the experience I had gained, and expanded it into an income-generating operation, making jewellery and other items using beads and recycled tyre rubber. The success we saw with the project was due in large part to my experience with April.

I ended up being evacuated when war broke out and it was no longer safe to stay. I returned briefly, then left again to get married and deal with some post-traumatic stress disorder. After going back one last time as a married couple to finish the work, we moved to Egypt to assist displaced refugees with job training, placement and education programmes. We dealt with some young people, but mostly with adults, the rationale being that if we could get adequate jobs for parents, we could help to keep their children off the streets.

Because of my health we had to move back to the USA after about two years, but I am still incredibly passionate about vulnerable people and children at risk. Living overseas obviously busted my world view wide open. I always wanted to go to the 'dark' and dangerous places and take them the light of God. But I actually found God was already there, where He always said He would be, among some of the most vulnerable people in the world. It is up to us to stand in solidarity with them, suffering with them and relieving what suffering we can.

Experiencing different cultures and perspectives helped me view things from outside that of just being an American middle-class Caucasian gal, and I'm better for it. Befriending street children, refugees, survivors of war, and my Muslim neighbours changed me. I expected it to, I'd hoped it would, and I'm so glad it did.

As my health recovers, I hope to be involved in the same sort of work for a long time to come. I also want to start working towards ways we can avoid having kids on the streets in the first place, and keeping families intact. My thanks to April Holden for giving a young, inexperienced girl with a lot of passion a chance to find her feet in the field and among her boys. I am so grateful![4]

The vocational skills acquired by the young people went a long way towards helping them find steady work, even though good jobs were scarce. Some graduates returned home to become their families' breadwinners. However, many came from dysfunctional families that didn't want the boys to live with them. One young man whose parents were dead was trying to live with an uncle who often got drunk and beat him. But he had nowhere else to go. He couldn't find work and he wanted to complete his education in the city. Some graduates found accommodation with the centres' staff members, but it was difficult even for them since prospective employers had a great deal of prejudice against boys who came from the streets.

In 2006 a record number of 20 boys between the ages of 14 and 18 were reconnected with relatives who were willing to accept them. This reflected the staff's success both in stabilizing the young people, physically and emotionally, and in finding reliable guardians. Some boys were able to leave because their fathers had returned from the war and were now supporting their families. Others went to live with relatives who weren't their parents, preparing to return to their home villages. All the boys who left faced big changes. Many would no longer be able to attend school, and their impoverished circumstances would mean eating a meal only once each day instead of three times, as they had at the centres.

Older teenagers who graduated and chose to travel back to distant villages didn't always communicate how they fared. This was always a disappointment to April and her co-workers, who continued to pray for each of them, knowing that some of the young people were the only Christians in their families or even tribes.

Sadly, one teenager with a learning disability who went to live with his brother in the capital was drafted into the army. The authorities refused to release him, insisting the boy would only work in the kitchen. But they sent him into the war zone, where he was shot and killed.

For a long time April had cherished a vision of renting a house that graduate boys could live in if they had no family or if they were in university and therefore needed to stay in the city. However, few benefactors had an interest in supporting boys once they became adults. A halfway house was finally opened in 2010 where older young men could live together with a staff member, slowly learning the life skills needed to function independently in society, such as working, budgeting and shopping.

When April's team opened a shop to help the young men learn responsible business practices, the group of businessmen that had helped them before generously gave advice and oversight. Their expertise made all the difference in changing failing initiatives into successes.

Young Peter was typical of the boys who were beginning once more to dream dreams.

> When I was small, there was no money and no food. My parents sent me to live with my big brother. I washed cars in the market and went home at night. I had no school, only work. Someone told me to try corn wine. I became addicted. I was always drunk and causing trouble for my brother. I used to sleep out in the streets and beg. I was in a bad way, begging door to door. I used to beg at April's house. She brought a teacher to ask me if I would go to live in the centre. I went with him, left all my bad ways and became a good student. I love to sit with the teachers and learn from the Bible and pray. I love mechanics. I want to be an architect and build big buildings.

As each boy matured and became more confident in living on his own, the team helped set him up in a trade or profession. Some were given metalwork or carpentry tools, others went to work in a factory or other job. Sponsors were found locally or in other countries for teenagers who did well scholastically, so they could continue their studies at college. The Centres of Love remained open to graduates on Saturdays so they could visit friends, staff members or brothers who were still living there. But learning to live independently was a difficult step for the boys.

'We made a mistake with our first set of graduates,' recalled April. 'They felt we had rejected them because in this culture, single people don't leave home until they are married. We learned a lot from their pain. After that we had a two-year preparation programme before graduation and then maintained good contact with them after graduation. The few boys that we know returned to the streets were from that first set of graduates, and we continued reaching out to them.'

Despite the high unemployment rate in the city, a sample survey of the centres' graduates showed that a good percentage managed to integrate successfully into normal society. Mason became a metalwork teacher at the second centre, Hafez joined the army and Luke got work as a traffic policeman. Christopher was an accountant. Three more graduates – Naji, Raif and Omari – earned a living as carpenters and mechanics, and three others became pilots. Abdul and Kafil worked in factories, Marco got a scholarship for secondary school and college. Another young man was accepted in a government scheme to study economics at Cairo University.

Eight other students were able to attend universities through the sponsorship of Christians in Hong Kong. One of them, Emmanuel, was the same boy who had once confided: 'My mother likes wine more than she likes me, and my father was also a drunkard. Because of this I ran away to the streets. The street provided me with food that people had thrown away from their tables. One day some teachers came to the street looking for lost children or for broken-hearted children. I was one of those children. So now I've found someone who can think of me as a human being, even show me the way to happiness. Inside of the centre, away from the streets, I found rest somehow and I knew there was hope. I came to believe that whatever is my life, there is Someone who respects that life and it is very expensive [valuable] in His eyes – because He made it.'

April was always thrilled when an unexpected gift gave one of her boys a fresh start. One British lady sent money in memory of her husband, enabling two graduates to take driving tests so they could get jobs as drivers. Another person helped a young man who wanted to start a small clothing store to support his family.

Shaun had been kidnapped from the far south as a small child, after his parents and other adults were killed. Along with other children he was forced into slavery. When he escaped to the capital city the staff at the centre had finally located an uncle, and Shaun went to live with him. Thanks to a donation from the UK he was able to make a living selling mobile phones and accessories from a kiosk.

The staff had no difficulty finding new boys to fill vacancies that came up at the centres. An endless stream of homeless waifs washed ashore on city streets, each child hoping to find work and a safe place to call home. The hard part was deciding which ones to take in. Ironically, a new law came into effect making it illegal for children to be on the streets. The police had launched a new campaign to remove all street people from the city and surrounding districts. Most ended up behind bars.

Young Jacob found his way to the second centre with spine and lungs damaged from tuberculosis of the spine, plus a heart condition. Against the odds he managed to complete the centre's educational programme. And although he didn't pass his final school exam he successfully trained as a metalworker. After accepting the Lord into his life Jacob changed from an angry, selfish teenager to a caring young man. He loved looking after the younger children, cutting their hair, ironing their clothes and giving gentle advice or correction. But later, after going to live at a house shared by older boys, his faith took a battering. He became depressed and his health deteriorated because he did not care for himself properly. The young man ended up in prison for a short time, charged with brewing alcohol.

The team were glad to welcome Jacob's subsequent return to the centre for rehabilitation, although he was very ill from deeply infected pressure sores that led to chronic osteomyelitis. A Christian in Hong Kong offered to pay his medical expenses, but no doctor seemed able to cure him. Jacob underwent surgery twice to close one of his wounds; both attempts were unsuccessful and the lesion reopened after a week. However, he was now in better spirits and his body was slowly responding to the unstinting care of the people around him. It was decided that once he was healed he should live permanently at the first Centre of Love, where he could help with the younger children.

Jacob proved a perfect fit for this work. The smaller boys respected the older young man who had survived such tough times. Eventually, when Christian ministries came under pressure and many closed, he took charge of the centre and remained committed to the boys. Few would guess that, years before, doctors gave this young man only three months to live! His Creator obviously had different plans.

April also marvelled at the case of Michael. This young man had run away from home when his mother suddenly attacked him with a knife, giving no explanation to her shocked and bewildered child. He turned up at the Centre of Love after two years on the streets.

Michael flourished in the loving atmosphere of his new home. Accepting the Lord into his life led to emotional healing, and one day he announced that he wanted to go back to help his family. The staff who made contact with them were never able to understand why the mother had attacked this son, since other siblings were still being cared for at home. Although they had no evidence, they guessed that Michael, the eldest, had been fathered by a man who wasn't the woman's husband, perhaps even an attacker. She never explained her aversion to the boy, and her husband was killed in the war, so he was not able to shed any light on the matter.

Michael was determined to return to his mother, and he did, but she attacked him again. The teenager came back to the centre in a terrible state. It took time and love for him to work through the hurt, but after he had grown up and trained as a police officer, he visited his mother faithfully. When she became very ill he was the one who took care of her, even though by then he had a wife and three children of his own. Later her condition worsened and her leg was amputated. Michael remained constant in the midst of his increasing family responsibilities. God gave him the grace to love and care for the woman who had twice tried to take his life.

Young Stephen got off to an unpromising start when his mother gave birth to him inside a prison. Later his father died and his step-father rejected him, so he drifted for several years before finding a safe haven at the centre. Stephen was sickly but a good boy, possessed of a loving disposition. He was prone to infections and had been diagnosed with tuberculosis three separate times, so he spent months in and out of the isolation hospital. When he was 17 his stepfather died; his mother took him and her other children to a village down in the south, which was then at peace.

The team heard nothing about Stephen for the next two years. Then the woman brought her son back to the centre with a swollen belly and clearly near death. The team put Stephen into hospital, and over the next six months they moved him to two other facilities where he received various treatments and blood transfusions. Finally they found a Coptic doctor who got to the bottom of his illness. It was a very difficult period. Some of the people belonging to the international church and school, who had the right blood type, donated blood for Stephen's transfusions. He underwent major surgery to remove his spleen and part of his liver. His mother was told that the boy would be on medication for the rest of his life and must never return to the more tropical south.

Hearing this warning, she quietly took her son's hand, then placed it into April's. 'I must return to my other children,' she told her sadly. 'He is your son now.'

April was shaken, but willingly shouldered the responsibility. What, she wondered, would the future hold for this young man who had already suffered so many years in the prison of his body? The team tried to find a way to get Stephen to a safer climate, but it was too difficult. Eventually he went to live with his young uncle, a deacon in the church on the outskirts of another town. He remains there still, and is prospering.

9

Green shoots in a dry land

See that you do not despise one of these little ones . . . your Father in heaven is not willing that any of these little ones should perish.
(Matthew 18.10, 14)

In time, the vocational training at the second centre expanded to include carpentry, car mechanics and metalwork, to supplement English classes, music, art, handicrafts and life skills. The boys attended a Catholic vocational training school nearby for other subjects. Although such instruction was indispensable, finding and retaining good teachers for the low salary offered was an ongoing challenge. A man teaching carpentry had financial troubles, so he kept disappearing to make money in his own workshop. At the same time a mechanics instructor proved to be too inexperienced and had to be replaced; an expatriate friend was temporarily filling in and giving oversight. A generator was acquired so the team could operate the metalwork programme on a daily basis, but then the electrical wiring burnt out. A German farmer overseas with whom April was in contact made tentative plans to assist with their agricultural programme and advise on how to work their farmland better.

Then a Swiss man and his wife joined the team. Bastien was a social worker and had a great deal of experience working with troubled teenagers and young adults. April was thrilled that Bastien and Raphael, a carpenter who also came from Switzerland, could assume overall responsibility for the teenagers. Bastien's wife Tina had administration skills, as well as some medical training, so she could step in to help with the younger boys.

April deeply appreciated all of the volunteers who served at the Centres of Love, whether they were able to give a few months or a few years. Each person made their own distinctive contribution – like Lily Matthews from the UK, who spent three years with the project:

I loved living in North Africa and it was an easy adjustment to move there. My first two years I was on a student visa as I was learning Arabic. I lived with some other female workers including April, until she moved to the adjoining house. A door between the two places made it easy to see her.

The people of this country are generally very warm, friendly and kind. I loved the food and hot weather, except sometimes when we had prayer meetings in a room with no fan. I have a strong memory of sweat running down my legs in streams . . . until I figured out how to dress more comfortably!

The only thing that really stressed me was the driving. I usually caught buses, but April had a lot of back problems, so one of the things I did to help was driving her places as smoothly as possible, which was very hard on bumpy roads. Especially challenging was driving on to bridges at the 'wrong time of day', when they were extremely crowded and everyone jostled to get on to the bridge.

I usually reached the older boys' centre by bus, which took about one and a half hours from the city. Often I went first to Arabic school. In the beginning I spent quite a bit of time with the boys and I was thankful that as a single person I was able to pick up some Arabic pretty quickly. Among my first words were: knife, problem, fight, thief, steal and glue!

Then April gave me more responsibility, so I did teacher training and helped the directors –first Jeffrey and then Job. They were both outstanding guys and it was a big privilege to work with them.

On Fridays the boys liked to play football (soccer) so I would go and be the audience, cheering them on. The field was a dust bowl next to a farm and a very bushy area.

One day three young men appeared out of the bushes while I was watching the boys play. The day before they had come to the centre armed with big knives or machetes, to ask for money. They knew that I was doing the books with the director every week and wanted to speak to me. They also said another boy there owed them money. So the staff told me and this boy to lock ourselves into the teachers' sleeping room, which we did, and eventually the boys were persuaded to go away. The ringleader was banned from the centre for aggressive, drunken behaviour and his refusal to behave in an appropriate way.

This second time, they came up to me very meekly. They had been fighting and were wounded. Since I had a first aid kit with me I bandaged them up. The boys were thankful. The next time I saw the ringleader he was drunk again; I often saw him drunk in the street and it was very sad. One time he beat up another lady worker from Brazil. With him and boys like him it was greatly comforting to know that God loved them more than we ever could and would give them every chance to turn to Him and be healed.

Other boys clearly changed during their time at the centre, wanting by God's grace to make the best of their lives. They did incredibly well too, given the backgrounds they had come from. Many showed enthusiasm for school and wanted to follow Jesus. Some were skilled at leading the others in singing. I really enjoyed worshipping with them.

I remember that we introduced a reward system. Boys with enough points got a reward on Friday, and one of the things I did with them was take them fishing. I am clueless about fishing, but I went to the market and got hooks and line, in the hope that the boys would know what to do with them. One found worms and we went down to the river a few times. It was a quick walk. I am sure as we passed the bricklayers they thought it was extremely strange to see a white woman walking there, especially with a bunch of teenage boys! They caught a fish at least once and in any case we had a nice time.

One year a big container came in with ski suits (salopettes or trousers and jackets) from Scandinavia! They were sold very cheaply after the boys all happily chose an outfit, despite it being usually about 32 °C (90 °F) and maybe down to 23 °C (75 °F) early in the morning, because it was winter. They loved wearing their jackets in the 'cold' weather!

I enjoyed the food at the centres. My favourite lunch dish (eaten at 3 p.m.) was a traditional vegetable broth like a sweet potato stew. The other staff introduced me to rice with sugar sprinkled on top. Sometimes a teacher would buy some sugar and we would have this as 'dessert', since usually there was only a main course.

The staff who worked at the centres day in day out were absolutely key. It was these men and women God primarily worked through to change the boys. Although they themselves usually came from poor, difficult backgrounds, they persevered, serving God by serving the boys. They all fulfilled the role of 'parents' and although like all of us they were not without fault, they were the salt and light the boys experienced day to day.

The ladies who mainly worked in the kitchen were the only females on the staff at the second centre, so they mothered the boys who, despite all being teenagers, really needed mothering. One woman had a daughter who became my good friend and we are still in contact via Facebook. I spent quite a bit of time with two staff members as well, and I am still friends with them.

Jacob was a former resident who had bad health and ended up in prison. When he got out of prison on Christmas Eve I spent my first Christmas Day morning in that country cleaning up his pressure sores and trying to make sure he would be comfortable until the next day. Jacob later became a faithful leader at the centre.

Sharing drinking cups was common in this culture. At the centre there was usually a water cooler with a cup attached that everyone used. But sometimes the water supply on the compound ran out. The climate is so hot and dry that being thirsty is very challenging. I didn't feel I could buy myself water to drink from a shop without buying it for everyone, and I couldn't afford that. So I went with the kitchen ladies sometimes to find a zeer, a clay pot with water in it that homeowners and businesses put outside their walls for people who need a drink. The boys used their own initiative to find water!

In this culture, relationship comes very much before task. Coming from a very task-orientated country, it was very easy to offend, completely unintentionally. It was always difficult to get the balance right. In a centre like the ones we ran there is clearly a place for structure and programme, but this needed to come after relationships. Looking back, I think the biggest thing I would do differently is focus from the very beginning on relating with the other staff.

During my third year I invited the teachers and their families over for food, one family at a time. It was usual to expect people to arrive an hour or so late. However, by the finish of the second hour you could assume they probably weren't coming. One time I started giving away the food I had cooked, only for the family to show up two and a half hours late! Thank-fully I had enough, although when they arrived I did have a moment's panic.

Committee meetings followed the same laid-back timetable. A meeting would be called and usually about half of the people would turn up. The next time maybe three-quarters came an hour or so late. The third meeting might actually take place as scheduled, albeit with someone missing because they had been unexpectedly held up.

In 2005 I got married and left to join a different organization in the country, and two years later my husband and I moved to a new house with our baby daughter. In the nearby market we saw a boy I knew from the centre, now in his early twenties. Jem was disabled and the boys had cruelly nicknamed him 'Monkey' because of the way he walked. He needed money, so we gave him some work helping to clean up our house. He also had a job as a guard at a building site. Jem had some problems and we were able to pray with him.

One night he came to us with a terrible cold and cough. I gave him medicine, and more importantly we prayed for him. God healed Jem and the next morning he was fine.

When the job as a guard didn't work out and he ended up with no place to sleep, we said Jem could stay in our yard if he wanted. (Most people sleep outside, because it's cooler. My first summer there I was house-sitting a friend's house and there was no air cooler; even if there was, electricity was dodgy. So I just slept outside.)

We hired Jem to do various jobs and had some really good times with him. He usually ate dinner with us in the late afternoon and we shared special days such as birthdays and Christmas. At the same time we encouraged him to actively look for work. Sometimes he found it, sometimes not. I don't know where this man is now. In hard times he did turn to God, so wherever he is my hope is that Jem is still trusting Jesus.

In 2011 my husband and I went to the USA for a year's furlough, but then we could not get visas to return.

Sometimes I like to remember the little sapling that I found growing in a friend's garden during my second year. I transplanted it to the middle of the 'yard' at the centre and we made a little garden. That little sapling eventually grew into a tree so big the staff held meetings and ate lunch under its branches. It provided shade and greenness in a brown land.

I think this is a picture of the changes we saw in our boys. Sometimes the change was drastic, as when I first planted that little tree and other green shrubs in the brown dirt. But often the changes were gradual – just like a growing tree. I guess that's how God changes all of us.

The sad reality of life in this country was that, as Jem mentioned above, not all of the children who found refuge at one of the Centres of Love had a happy-ever-after ending. One year, 55 of the boys who regularly dropped into the centre were taken away by police and put into government reform schools. They were all under the age of 12. This was a great blow to the staff. Yet within a week the same number of boys were coming for food at the centre, proof of the endless flow of children who scavenged on the streets.

Moses would have counted himself among the lucky ones:

My parents separated when I was very small. My mother went very far away and left me with my grandmother. After a while my grandmother sent me to my mum. When I was there she beat me badly and sent me back to my grandmother in the capital, but I lost my way and could not find her. [Unbelievably, Moses was only four years old at the time he was sent alone on this very long journey.]

I stayed living on the streets. I was sad and crying, looking through a fence at a house. I didn't have enough clothes. I was sleeping in the rain. One day a car hit me when I crossed the street. There was nobody to help me. I got to the hospital and they put some bandages on me and sent me away. My legs were not broken but I was hurt and my head hurt.

I was very angry inside. I was fighting with a boy on the street as well. I was weeping because I was on the street. Then one day I made a friend. We went to swim in the river and it was fun. We were smoking. I was dreaming I would have a car one day. I did not know where my family was. I sniffed glue to try to forget.

One day, after I had been on the streets for a while, I met another boy. He took me to the centre. I found friends in the centre. I could go to school for the first time ever and now I know how to read and write. I watch TV and have fun with my friends. I love being in the centre with my friends and teachers. When I grow up I would like to be a doctor and to have a wife and children. My children will go to school and watch TV.

Moses lived happily at the first centre from the age of six until he was twelve. The staff looked for the boy's family, but his mother and grandmother had both disappeared. Moses' father, who had also been on the streets, hadn't been seen for years.

Then, suddenly, Moses went missing on his way home from school, just two blocks from the centre. The police and everyone else searched for him; his photo was placed in the newspaper, even on TV, to no avail. April and the other caregivers were distraught. How could a little boy just vanish?

Three years later Moses reappeared, ragged, bone thin and

severely traumatized. The boy said he had gone with a man who claimed to be his father. After being taken to a distant place he was introduced to a lady he was told was his mother. Moses didn't recognize either of the adults and he was treated as a slave.

One day he managed to escape and somehow found his way back, in stages, to the centre. It took a great deal of time and care before he felt secure and well again. Fearing that Moses would be found by his kidnappers, a staff member took him into his own home. The police knew he was back and approved the arrangement as the boy was no longer a child.

Arif and his family lived in the far west of the country before moving to the capital city. The boy learned how to earn money as a shoe-shiner on the city streets each day, returning home each evening. Then one day when he was out working, one of his friends who lived on the street asked him to go along with him to the market. Arif went and was taught how to beg and steal. This seemed a more profitable and adventurous way to make money. Sometimes he stole plastic bags and vegetables, and sold them. He used his money to buy food and cigarettes, and picked up many other bad habits from the boys he hung out with.

One day some teachers from the centre visited the market and met Arif. When they invited the ten-year-old to live with the other boys, he accepted immediately. Arif spent the next four or so years there and in 2003, when he turned 14, transferred to the second centre.

During the Christmas holidays that year, while Arif was visiting relatives, soldiers forcibly recruited the boy and put him into what was believed to be a terrorist training camp. The director of the centre requested permission to visit him, but was refused access. At only 14 years of age, Arif was now a child soldier in the army. Not even his family were allowed to see him.

Under the laws of war, the recruitment or use of children under 15 by parties involved in a conflict is a war crime. However, children as young as 7 or 8 (though more often aged 10 to 17) have been forcibly recruited for decades, particularly for fighting in the south part of the country. Many child soldiers were among the two million who died during the civil war.

Hundreds of child soldiers were released in 2004, as part of efforts to establish peace. However, in spite of the passing of a 2008 Child Act that established a minimum age of 18 for any conscription or voluntary recruitment into armed forces, the practice still continues. The United Nations International Children's Emergency Fund (UNICEF) estimates that in the last five years 15,000 to 16,000 children may have been used by armed forces and groups in this North African country.

'They said we must join the army. If not they would beat us,' related one boy interviewed for a Human Rights Watch report that detailed a government army recruitment drive. Another 15-year-old soldier remembered, 'We defeated and killed a lot of people . . . We were shooting, me and the other young kids. We were afraid but we had to do it anyway.'

No one really knows exactly how many children were torn from families and schooling, underfed, injured and traumatized by seeing friends killed in the fighting. 'When we were moving and boys got sick and died they would just be left where they fell,' reported one 14-year-old. Most children could not find their way home even if they were freed.[5]

With so many boys disappearing from the streets to serve as soldiers or put into reform schools with appalling conditions, April was anxious to expand the number they could take in as residents. In fact, the whole staff felt a growing urgency to rescue more of the country's homeless children, particularly in hotspots where the need was greatest. At the same time they knew the only way this could happen was by more local churches joining the effort, perhaps even setting up their own projects. Yet a major mobilization of churches would require dozens more facilitators who were specifically trained in development work.

April was grateful for the good relationship she and her ministry enjoyed with local fellowships. The Church was in many ways strong in prayer and outreach. In some places, believers boldly proclaimed their faith even though they were targeted for persecution. But of course no body of believers was perfect. Greater unity needed to be developed between the different tribal congregations and denominations. They were also hindered by a shortage of mature, godly leaders. The Church had experienced very rapid growth over a relatively short period of time, leaving thousands of young, new Christians without adequate teaching about discipleship.

It was also true that the Church was predominantly made up of very poor believers who struggled to feed even their own families. Church members were trying to help rebuild all the churches burned down or damaged during the war, as well as their own homes and communities. The state of this country after so many years of merciless conflict, not to mention the toll taken by floods, drought and disease, was too terrible for words.

Despite many delays and postponements, however, a long-awaited peace accord between opposing forces was finally signed. April wrote to friends:

> People are looking forward to peace with cautious optimism. The long, devastating war has torn ruthlessly into the lives of just about every family. Pray for forgiveness and for unity, especially among the tribes as well as among previous enemies.
>
> Also pray for future vision. Our work must change as people return to their towns and villages. The land has thousands upon thousands of orphans and homeless children as a result of war, poverty and AIDS. There will be a great need for wide-scale outreach to these children, helping them physically and spiritually. In addition to this, the whole infrastructure of half the country needs to be rebuilt, including schools and hospitals. We are praying about being involved in the establishment of Christian schools and also working with the orphans, sick and homeless children. It is an overwhelming prospect – hard to know even where to start, but God is able, and will give wisdom to us as we seek His will for our work. What seems impossible for us is possible for God.

It was a small miracle that their three Centres of Love had managed to survive the years of instability. April had first begun to reach out to street boys in 1996, but because the official opening of their facility wasn't until the following year, she agreed that the Centre of Love's tenth anniversary should be celebrated on 20 April 2007.

And what a joyful occasion it was! Former and current residential boys, as well as children the staff worked with on the streets, took part in the milestone event. Even some of the boys from the far south travelled to the capital to present their carefully prepared testimonies, songs and dramas. Church leaders and friends who had been part of the ministry in some way over the years were happy to contribute an abundance of sweets, fruit, dates and cakes. Everyone joined in giving praise to the Lord for all that had been accomplished.

At the end of the programme, the staff presented April with a beautiful wooden carving depicting an African mother. One little child was strapped to the woman's back and a second toddler stood by her feet, clinging to her skirt.

'An African mother for our Mama April,' the team smilingly told their speechless leader. The carving became one of April's most treasured possessions. Years later, when she was forced out of the country, the statue was the first thing she packed, in spite of its awkward size and weight. The gift meant far more to her than words could express.

10

A country divided

You, LORD, hear the desire of the afflicted; you encourage them, and
you listen to their cry, defending the fatherless and the oppressed,
so that mere earthly mortals will never again strike terror.

(Psalm 10.17–18)

A new and horrific chapter in African history began in 2003 with the
mass slaughter of men, women and children in the western region of
April's adoptive country. The United Nations eventually proclaimed
this development as one of the worst nightmares in recent history.
Even the most news-oblivious of people worldwide were shocked
into awareness of the genocide, even if they still weren't quite sure
where it was.

The people of this dusty area about the size of Spain were mostly
non-Arab Africans. For years they had suffered the consequences of
war, famine and destitution without any help from the government.
Then oil was discovered under their sandy soil, and the region suddenly became a matter of national interest. Competition to claim
the underground wealth finally pushed rebel groups into attacking a
government air base.

This move triggered violent retribution. A group of armed Arab
militias swept into the villages and began systematically burning
homes, looting economic resources, polluting water sources, and
murdering, raping, castrating and torturing innocent civilians. Over
the next few years hundreds of thousands of people died and some
three million others were displaced from their homes. More children
wandered alone on the streets than could be numbered.

Although April lived far away from them, she yearned to do
something to help these desperate boys and girls. A foreigner going

there would be too conspicuous, so she asked her co-worker Jeffrey – now the overall director of the Centres of Love – to take emergency aid to the children. Jeffrey was just recovering from typhoid, but willingly travelled to the area to coordinate the relief efforts and help establish a feeding centre.

Blankets, warm clothes, food supplies and cooking utensils were gladly received by a small local church, which undertook to distribute blankets and clothes to street children to help protect them during the very cold weather. They also prepared brown-bean (*ful*) sandwiches and distributed them from the feeding centre to about 100 children each day. Jeffrey and other team members transported very sick children to the clinic, paying for their medical care. The children ate a good meal each day and stayed for lessons in Arabic, English and mathematics, glad to escape the streets for at least a short while longer. The young people from the church worked tirelessly and entirely without pay, even though they themselves had so little.

April longed to build a separate facility to relieve the pressure on the church, which only had a tiny compound with two rooms and a yard. The new building would function like the kind of day centre she had first established, where children could get emergency counselling, food, first aid and education. However, when others urged her team to open another Centre of Love in this troubled area, she knew they just didn't have the means. In fact, their existing centres were struggling to cope with a financial shortage for the second year running. They had been unable to accept any new boys, and a few faithful staff members had even had to be let go. Daily meals were temporarily cut down from three to two – which was still more than many people in this country had to subsist on – but it was not a situation April wanted for her boys.

Then, unexpectedly, a large donation came in, specifically designated for a new centre. April and her co-workers rejoiced, and consulted with World Orphans, a ministry empowering churches that wanted to help homeless children. A partnership was born.

The local government had already fully approved the church's outreach to street boys in two rented rooms. It even contributed a piece of land for building a proper centre. So World Orphans started construction of a group home and multi-purpose facility to be used as a church hall and school for 20 of the youngest and most needy boys aged 12 and under. A caregiver family would live with them. A second group home would hopefully be added later to accommodate more homeless children.

Initially, April hadn't been sure how long such a project would survive because of the area's instability. Even with the provision of land, building on it had seemed like an impossible dream. However, the Lord in His compassion made a way where there seemed to be no way. Monthly funds were pledged to totally support the first year of operation, with lesser amounts over the next five years until the local church was able to take over.

Meanwhile, in July 2007 the UN Security Council approved a resolution authorizing a 26,000-strong peacekeeping force for the beleaguered territory. World Orphans finished construction of the new Centre of Love by the end of that year. Teachers bought furniture, books and sets of clothing for the new boys, determined to get them out of the cold weather by Christmas. When the official opening was finally held the next month, young and old came together to celebrate with singing, drama and games. It was a wonderful triumph in the midst of so much despair. Although the church gave thanks for this new ministry, April knew it would be no small task for them to take on the raising and rehabilitation of troubled boys, even with Jeffrey giving oversight.

'In the beginning the boys told us many lies,' he reported. 'But after the teachers worked with them about loving one another and they got to know their teachers, they stopped telling lies. They told us the truth about their families. This enabled us to find and contact relatives.'

When one of the mothers located by the staff took her son away, not wanting Monty to stay at the centre, he ran away from her and climbed on top of a train to escape. Tragically, the boy fell off the train and lost his leg. During his hospital stay an uncle and aunt came from far away and announced they were going to raise the child in their family. They had not known he was on the streets or that his mother wasn't caring for him properly. Monty was very happy to go with them, even though he now had to adjust to living with a disability.

Jeffrey wrote:

Most of the boys are settled now. They are happy to not be on the streets and to have the opportunity to be in school. One day the teachers took the boys for a picnic and they went swimming in the river. Before they swam, the teacher told them he would pray with them for God to keep them safe. When one of the boys was swimming, something caught his foot. He was being dragged down when two teachers who were nearby saved him. Then, on the way back, the teacher who was in charge suddenly felt that something was wrong. He shouted, 'Stop! Stop!' Everyone stopped and they saw in front of them a snake hiding inside a plastic bag. A man stood across the street, watching. When the teacher started to kill the snake the man shouted at him. He looked the man in the eyes and shouted back. The stranger ran away, so he killed the snake. When they got home some of the boys told the teacher, 'When you pray we are always kept safe, Papa.'

Neighbours in town were not sure about how to take the centre at first, but as they saw the good work the church was doing they began to send their children to play with the boys. Good relationships were promoted by opening night schools for the adults and after-school classes for the neighbourhood children. The night schools also provided a small income for the centre. In the end, the area leaders backed the church's efforts and protected it from harassment. A teacher was sent from the government security office to ensure that Muslim boys were not forced to become Christians, but the children who were Christians were excited about what they learned in Sunday school. God knit the boys – former strangers or rival gang members – into a family, the older ones taking care of the younger.

One critical objective of the centre was to link the children back to their families if they still existed, so that if and when the fighting ended they could go home. This was not viable for boys whose parents were still caught somewhere inside the war zone; their families could only be traced after a ceasefire. However, if the parents had settled in displaced refugee camps it was possible to find them. Although the staff sometimes compared their search to looking for needles in haystacks, the sweet satisfaction that came from reuniting families was well worth the effort.

One of the children was rescued by the police when he was two years old because his mother was mentally disturbed. The church found someone to help the mother and cared for the boy. At one point they tried to reunite the two, but the woman tried to attack the toddler. He was so traumatized the believers took him back and Hassan and his wife, who lived at the centre, treated him as their own son.

Another time a 12-year-old resident went to visit his uncle, who had only recently been located. The man was an imam (Muslim cleric). 'Uncle,' the boy told him earnestly, 'you need to divide your mosque into two – half for the Christians and half for the Muslims – because the Christians also need to pray.' His uncle just smiled and agreed, 'Yes, they also need to pray.'

Jeffrey described the joyful reunion of a boy with his lost family, and how his face shone as he said his goodbyes to everyone at the centre: 'I am so happy that I found my parents! They are Christians – they came here because of war. Thank you to all of you for all my time in the Centre of Love, for encouragement to go to church and pray all the time, remembering God as my family taught me.'

Jeffrey reported that the parents had subsequently moved south. They had refused to go back until they found all their children, and were jubilant to have their lost son restored to them.

Meanwhile, the tug of war over the region raged on. When government planes bombed rebel positions, some areas became no-go zones for aid workers. It was a blow when a number of major organizations were either forced to leave or voluntarily pulled out in order to protect their staff. Local people employed by these groups suddenly found themselves jobless, which in turn led to some of them losing their homes. For the thousands who were dependent on the organizations for basic food, shelter and medical care, this development was nothing short of catastrophic.

Thankfully, because local churches took ownership of the Centre of Love, the rescue and rehabilitation of street children in the west was able to continue. However, the efforts of teachers trying to trace relatives became more problematic.

April was facing her own set of challenges as the whole country underwent serious political upheaval. Following years of conflict, the Arab and Christian populations in the north and south finally agreed on establishing independent governments.

Since the media were reporting that threats and rioting had broken out on the streets, April and the other staff members prayed about their situation. They decided it would be unwise to keep large groups of southern children together in one compound. Even though the boys would miss school they would be safer temporarily redistributed among extended family members or church families from their own tribes. Church members were on standby to whisk the children to safety if they were threatened. The three boys whose only families were in the south were sent down to the third Centre of Love. Teachers from the two capital city-based centres escorted all of the children to their temporary homes and left them with two weeks' supply of dry foodstuff. This could be replenished when needed; stores of food were routinely kept at the centres in case something happened to close down the markets. Half of the staff who had roots in the south also took their families there. Those who remained guarded the centres and kept in contact with the boys, telephoning and visiting families to ensure that everyone was being adequately cared for.

During the next year there was a dramatic population shift as many people who had been displaced, living in the north, made immediate plans to be repatriated to the south. This affected April's ministry, because a number of the boys who had been living in the centres had to move with their relatives; they couldn't stay on without them. This meant the staff had to ascertain which adults were stable enough to take the boys. Even those who had graduated and were still in the capital decided to migrate with immediate or extended family and tribal members. Displaced members of April's own team joined the general exodus. She organized a retreat for everyone on the staff to gather for one last time to commit the future to the Lord and exchange farewells.

Soon only 25 boys were left in the first and second centres, and only five of these at the time were northerners. Then newspapers announced that the authorities were making a list of southern children staying in homeless shelters in the north. These children would be deported. With the government's intentions clear, it was obvious that the 20 southern children still living at the capital-based Centres of Love could no longer remain.

As soon as the school term ended that February, arrangements were made to conduct the boys to safety in the south. They went in groups with church members of the same tribe or team members' families. April had decided they should reopen temporary drop-in programmes at centres one and two. This move would serve several purposes. The staff would be able to meet new southern children at the centres or out wandering the streets; they could then try to link them with their families, so that relatives did not repatriate without them. They could also find ways to help children whose families had already departed, assuming their sons or daughters had died as it had been so long since they'd seen them.

Next, staff would make contact with homeless northern children and assess the possibility of having them stay at the centres. Hopefully the government would allow the church to continue running those projects.

As time went on it became increasingly plain that Christians were no longer welcome to remain in the north. Although most displaced families wished to be repatriated and reclaim their ancestral lands, hundreds of thousands of southerners found themselves stranded without visas, money or transport. The logistical problems were enormous. Some owned homes, farms and shops in the north and didn't know what would become of their property. Conditions in the south were primitive; it was possible that nothing at all remained of their former homes and villages. Yet staying on as foreigners in the north might prove even more dangerous.

The dramatic shift of the nation's population was bound to have profound spiritual repercussions. Christians who had fled the beleaguered south years before had planted many churches near their new homes. Now these churches were emptying as the government stepped up the pressure, picking up foreign and national Christians for questioning. Some men and women were imprisoned and some deported. Churches were closed, missions forced to leave. April prayed that God would have His way in her own future, and that the light of Christ would not be snuffed out as the new regime pushed for a strict enforcement of Islam.

Meanwhile, the south was desperately trying to cope with the tidal wave of refugees pouring in from the north. Most new arrivals stayed in makeshift camps or transit areas, waiting to be transported to their final destination. They had little to live on. One of April's team members tearfully described how refugee families were forced to cut branches and cover them with sheets, blankets or cardboard to provide some sort of shelter during the wet season. They had arrived with the hope of being housed, many even bringing furniture, but found themselves camping in fields, without the means to go further. Others who did reach their home areas found them completely destroyed and didn't know where to turn. A doctor known to the team had been unable to sell his house in the capital, so he just had to leave it, taking his family and all the money he possessed. He used up his savings simply trying to survive for four months, and his family became destitute.

Local governments and aid agencies were overwhelmed by the numbers facing insufficient housing and limited or no water and food supplies. Much of the south had no roads, piped water, electricity, clinics or schools. Many communities were struggling to run schools under trees, without books or slates. More children than ever begged for food on the streets. It would take years to develop the most basic infrastructure.

April and her staff had asked the families who took their boys south to let them know how they fared. They heard from only three. They could only pray daily that the families would find homes, provide adequately for the children and continue their education. Most of all, they prayed the boys would not forget God's love.

Meanwhile there were still thousands of children on the streets of the capital city who were in urgent need of rescue. Drop-ins were welcomed for several months, both boys and girls. All received a balanced meal, a place to wash, counselling and schooling, as well as recreational sports and games. Then the facility reverted back to full-time residential care for 12 new permanent residents from the streets, aged from 6 to 14. They were in rough physical condition and in even rougher shape emotionally, quick to act out their aggression. One boy in particular kept trying to sneak glue into the centre. But the newcomers gradually relaxed as they settled into a structured routine. Besides the unbelievable luxury of regular meals, they experienced fun activities, craft-making sessions and opportunities to learn. Thanks to donations, the compound's old bamboo classrooms were finally rebuilt with sturdy brick and cement, then fully furnished and equipped.

The plan had been to take in enough new boys over the summer of 2011 to fill up both of the centres. Tragically, however, at least 80 children living in the market area died from an unknown source of poisoning. Afterwards the police made a sweep of survivors, putting a large number into reform schools or children's prisons. The rest went into hiding. This made it impossible for the staff to contact new street kids, as they reacted with fear if anyone tried to approach. For a while there were only 17 living in the first centre and 20 in the second. By the end of the year, however, the total of residents had almost doubled.

New teachers had been found to replace the ones who had moved south, but they required training in how to work with emotionally disturbed children. The newcomers also needed to learn teaching methods other than the rote memorization commonly used in local schools. Another lack was vocational workshop teachers for the teenagers' centre.

Down in the south, churches were doing what they could to relieve the suffering of those displaced people who were returning. The Centre of Love located there was full to capacity and staff were seeking help from local sources to develop another piece of land, which would be reclaimed by the authorities if not built upon in the near future. Or else they could add another dormitory to the old property to accommodate more children.

Fighting still raged in the nearby mountains, which caused tension in the town. The centre's distance from the other branches of the street kids' ministry caused many practical problems and Samuel, the director, felt cut off. Roads used to transport supplies were no longer safe. As a result the price of sugar, salt, wheat and other dry staples skyrocketed at three to five times their normal cost. Meat, when it was available, was prohibitively expensive, and with the great river in flood, fish was even more costly than meat. Fortunately, vegetables and fruit could be locally grown or purchased during the wet season.

Uncertainty over the future persisted into 2012. Hostilities between north and south continued to break out. By this time Samuel had even lost telephone communication with the capital city, so he was forced to travel to another town every other week to stay in touch. The rains that year brought flooding and an increase in misery and disease to the south. But a new dormitory had been completed at the old property to accommodate the extra boys sent from the northern centres, and they were well and happy. April increased their budget to help with escalating costs.

Then, as if the situation in the north wasn't tense enough, a few pastors from one denomination began stirring discord over church property sales. These men also objected to some southern pastors still living in the north. Unfortunately they brought in the civil authorities, who ended up ruling that all southern pastors and elders from every denomination had to leave and go to the south. The troublemakers were dismissed, but by then it was too late. The testimony of Christians had been damaged and government officials had been given an opportunity to interfere with the internal affairs of the Church.

In addition to the disastrous loss of pastors and elders, all land and assets of the denomination were frozen. Unless disputes were solved, the authorities would confiscate everything. This could have serious repercussions for the Centres of Love, since three out of the four were on frozen church property. April pleaded with God for His intervention.

That spring, the church's property next to the second centre was attacked. They owned a large compound and only a section of it had been allocated to the street boys' work. Fortunately, this part was spared when an angry mob of hundreds marched from the local mosque one day and did extensive damage to the Bible school and church building, along with housing for students and pastors. Much was lost, but thankfully nobody was hurt. Although some Muslim neighbours wanted to take ownership of the compound, others – and even government officials – apologized for what had happened.

The court finally ruled that the property legally belonged to the church – as did the boys' section of the property. April's prayers had been answered. With the ownership issue settled, the staff were able to accept more boys into residential care.

April's church celebrated Easter in early April 2012 with a sunrise service on the beach by the river. Afterwards they shared a picnic lunch and held games for the little ones. In some ways, April reflected, Easter was even more meaningful to Jesus' followers than Christmas, for it marked the triumphant fulfilment of His mission on earth. It was a day she would long remember, even though she had no way of knowing at the time that it was to be her last Easter sunrise observance in her adopted country.

Following a quick trip to Germany to attend a relief and development conference that May, April visited the UK to speak and attend to various obligations until the end of June. Returning to Africa that September she was gratified by the church's new programme to assist destitute mothers and their families.

Around the end of October, the authorities confiscated April's passport. She was still working part time at a private school run by Christians, which the government wanted to shut down. At first officials ruled that Valley School would have to close immediately; then they decided it could stay open until May, the end of the school year. However, expatriate teachers knew they were living on borrowed time; they could be picked up and deported any day, at the whim of the government. One of April's friends was already in prison. Others had been questioned by security and given only 48 hours to leave. So she began to meet with church leaders and members of her staff, trying to get the Centres of Love organized so they could carry on if she had to leave suddenly.

Esther had by this time worked with April for 17 years. In addition to directing the first centre, she now became the family liaison teacher, spending much of her time visiting the boys' families. Her ambition was to work with mothers and hopefully find ways to successfully reunite them with their children. A male staff member accompanied Esther whenever a father was present, and other teachers also continued their visits.

April's difficulties were compounded that November when she fell and hurt her back. Then she came down with laryngitis and bronchitis while half of her school contracted whooping cough! In

December, two more of her colleagues were detained for questioning. One was given 48 hours to leave the country with his wife. The other man was subjected to many days of harsh interrogation before he too was deported. This left April as the only foreigner working with the boys and related church groups. She was suddenly without a bookkeeper, as well as the art teacher who had been helping her with communications. Her workload increased drastically and an auditor was due very soon to go over the books.

At the same time, April received news from her sister in England that their father was not doing well. He was suffering from dementia, which had suddenly taken a turn for the worse and he was now undergoing assessment in a residential home. April was distressed; a thousand questions about what this would mean in the future crowded her heart.

Meanwhile, the area where the fourth centre was located was experiencing sporadic unrest. The work had so far been protected, but the small church there was facing many financial pressures, including an extremely high rent. It was a struggle for the staff and their families to manage, even after making cutbacks. However, the new boys they had taken in were responding positively and anticipating Christmas – some of them for the first time.

The boys in the south had endured their own tough times through a rainy season bringing much flooding, but not even a deluge could dampen their spirits when it came to Christmas celebrations! Boys were the same everywhere, their brothers at the first and second centres up north also caught up in holiday excitement as they prepared the usual nativity play and festive programme for friends and family.

April was happily surprised when a member of her family gifted her with funds for a week's holiday in Ethiopia. Miraculously, the authorities allowed her to temporarily reclaim her passport, so on Boxing Day she and a friend departed for a night's stay in a lakeside guest house followed by days in a lodge surrounded by a lovely garden. The pair explored famous historical sites nearby and enjoyed a much-needed rest. Seen in retrospect, the week was clearly the provision of their merciful Lord, who knew what lay ahead.

'It is good to look back on 2012 and see many blessings,' April shared in an end-of-year letter to prayer partners. 'The children and staff are all doing well. We have ridden many a storm, experiencing God's help and presence in new and deeper ways. The church has begun a new ministry for destitute women. God has blessed us with good people on our team. We look forward to 2013, excited to see what God is going to do next. Life is never dull!'

The New Year got off to a hectic start as April worked with the auditor to close the financial year, trained and met with staff. Emotions were running high among the workers at both centres and the school. Then, on 24 January 2013, her world was turned upside down.

She happened to be in the classroom, teaching at Valley School, when the telephone call came. Later, as she read the message to call back, she hesitated. It wasn't a number she recognized. April later asked herself if she could have delayed the inevitable if she had simply ignored that call.

She did not. The voice that answered her ring identified himself as an officer with the national central security division. April was ordered to report to his office the next morning for questioning.

11

A future and a hope

Let the morning bring me word of your unfailing love, for I have put my trust in you. Show me the way I should go, for to you I entrust my life.
(Psalm 143.8)

Security officers finished interrogating April on the second day of February 2013. They had kept at her, shouting and threatening, from 9 a.m. to 9 p.m. Then they had sent her to another man, who demanded names of people she worked with. When she still refused to give them, they told her she was going to prison. Shortly after that, they ordered her deportation on a flight scheduled to take off in two hours. Her car had been confiscated, but God mercifully provided a taxi driver to take her home. At the house she found some of the staff and boys from the centres waiting outside to say goodbye. Other friends insisted on accompanying her to the airport. Her bags were already packed with her most precious possessions from the past 17 years – small tokens from friends and co-workers – crammed into the 46-kilo baggage allowance. Arrangements had been made for her beloved old dog Lady to go to a family at the Japanese embassy. They had promised to take good care of her.

At the airport, April sat tensely in the departure lounge before boarding her plane, fully expecting the police to turn up at any moment and snatch her away. But once again the Lord surrounded her with His care. Her fellow passengers, though they were total strangers, noticed the pale woman who looked so obviously nervous and unwell, and helped her with her bags. They were to renew their kindness at the other end, making sure she connected with the people who had come to meet her.

Finally April was allowed inside the departing aircraft, and after another interminable wait it lifted off the runway. As she watched the landscape of Africa recede from view, sadness and shock ravaged her heart. The abrupt severance from her friends and co-workers – and most of all her beloved boys – was almost too much to take in. What would become of them all? Why was God permitting this to happen?

She couldn't help the anxious thoughts that came flooding in, as well, about decisions awaiting her in England regarding her father's condition. How would she cope? How much care would he need? Where would she live?

Back on English soil, she was warmly welcomed by friends Ed and Pauline Clay. April understood that it was not possible for her sister Susan to meet her, as she lived some distance away and was unwell after dealing with their father. The Clays drove April to the mission base for three weeks of debriefing, then she spent a further week resting and relaxing in Scotland. Taking temporary accommodation in her aunt's sheltered housing unit after that, she looked for a longer-term place to live close to her father, who was by then in a nursing home.

When decision-making and logistics proved too much for April in her exhausted state, her sister and brother-in-law urged her to accept the sanctuary of their home. The unstinting generosity of this couple played a big part in her healing over the next months, as did close friends and a caring pastor. Yet at first April was so emotionally and physically shattered that she was like a broken-winged bird, lacking the heart to sing. She was convinced that she had failed God. The mission He had sent her to accomplish was far from fulfilled. Surely He hadn't intended for her to abandon the boys He had entrusted to her?

Later, April described how the Lord ministered to her through an elderly speaker at a Spring Harvest conference she attended in Minehead, on the Bristol Channel.

> I listened to this man share about how he delighted over his grand-children, and how, when they made mistakes, he cheered them on and encouraged them to keep going.

'Do we think we are better parents than God?' he challenged us. 'God alway delights in us and encourages us to keep going, even when we fail.'

I was so touched by this reminder of the Father's love that I went out and danced on the beach by the conference centre. God lifted me up and put joy back into my heart. Later, I had long chats with the Lord as I regularly took the six-hour bus drive between my sister's home and my father's residence. He even used the beauty of creation around me to touch my tired soul. I was able to accept my failures and remember the things that had gone well, and move on. As He taught me more about Himself, I learned more about myself.

Slowly news trickled in from North Africa. Persecution of the Church was increasing, with many local believers being subjected to arrest, imprisonment and torture. A couple of hundred foreign Christians had been expelled during the first months of 2013. Among them was a personal friend of April, who had been held in prison for 33 days.

As for the work among the boys, the older boys' centre had to be closed, although the buildings were still being used by the church. Many of the young people went to live in the south, where they seemed to be adjusting. This centre was fully operational, being run by the local church and Samuel in partnership with Mission 21, which had long been linked with the work.

The first Centre of Love in the capital was also still functioning under the church's auspices, with others helping as much as possible until local partners could be found. Although the boys were very naturally shaken by all the changes, homes had been found for many of those who were left. A number of staff members, including Esther, had to be let go to conserve funds, so Jacob took responsibility for the boys on the compound. Several church leaders were being called in daily for questioning.

Distressed by the collapse of the team and loss of her job, adding to the struggle to make ends meet for her large family, Esther decided to study for a degree in business administration. Her husband, who had studied for a theological degree in Jordan, taught part time at a theological college.

The fourth facility in the west kept going for a while after April left; later on the church members were imprisoned and one of the leaders vanished entirely.

April was able to maintain online communication with some of the older boys and her friends. Although she was not involved with the work any longer it was a comfort to keep in touch on a personal level. She was deeply encouraged, on Mother's Day that March, to receive emails from two of 'her' boys.

As anxious as she was about the children and staff she had left behind, April knew that she had to trust her heavenly Father, who loved them infinitely more. Gradually she received God's reassurance that her years in North Africa would not be wasted. Moreover, He still had work for her to do. Jeremiah's plea in Lamentations 2.19 rang in her heart even more loudly and clearly than ever: 'Cry out in the night, as the watches of the night begin; pour out your heart like water in the presence of the Lord. Lift up your hands to him for the lives of your children, who faint from hunger at every street corner.'

I am on a spiritual journey, she thought to herself. *God has put me in the fire. He has told me to wait on Him, that He is doing a new thing. I can respond to trial with self-pity or I can respond by focusing on God and allowing the fire of testing to make me stronger in my faith.*

Mission leaders insisted that after 20 years in ministry, April needed to take a full year's sabbatical. Her health was up and down, and although her overall condition had much improved she was still tired and suffered frequent headaches. So she took time out to pursue a fitness programme at the gym, learned to cycle, enjoyed crafts, helped with her church's Sunday school and spent quality moments with friends. For the first time in 20 years, she celebrated an English Christmas with her family.

Ever eager to develop the interest closest to her heart, April also signed up for an online diploma course in Community Transformation Project Design. But a good deal of that year was devoted to praying about where to go next. That she would continue to work somewhere in Africa was a given, but as April had said half-humorously to God years before, 'Africa is a big place. Could You be more specific?'

One day she decided to browse the web pages about Africa posted by OM International. April noticed that the country of Zambia was highlighted in the menu. She clicked on it and read about the projects in that country. A few days later when she returned to the website, Zambia was highlighted again. Her curiosity was piqued. OM seemed to have a great many ministries on that continent. Was God trying to tell her something? She closed the website, reopened it, and saw no country highlighted. Then she prayed, 'OK, Lord, if You want me to focus on Zambia, then highlight it the next time!' She switched off her computer. When she opened the Africa site once more, there it was: Zambia, coloured in bold letters for her attention.

April did more research about this nation embedded in the south-central heart of the continent, and asked others to pray with her. It just didn't seem to make sense. Zambia was more than 80 per cent Christian!

'Father, why would You want me to go to a Christian country?' she finally asked. 'They should be sending missionaries, not receiving them!'

'Exactly,' was the answer God dropped into her mind and heart.

April began to comprehend that He wasn't asking her to do the same work that she had done before. During her years in North Africa it had been patently obvious that she could never set up enough projects to help all the endangered children. The answer then – and still was – to equip local churches to get involved. If God, the Father of the fatherless, lit a fire in His people and they became families for the fatherless, there would be no limits to what could be accomplished.

The fact of the matter was that few of the many thousands of churches spread across Africa were working with children and young people who lived full time on the streets. Age-old barriers of fear, stigmas and false beliefs stood rock solid. Once believers could be made to see these vulnerable children as part of their God-given responsibility, they would be open to training.

As April thought about the possibilities, her excitement grew. God's plans were so much bigger than her own! If motivating and empowering Christians was truly His purpose for her, using Zambia as a springboard made perfect sense. The country was centrally located, and its many churches were in a position to contribute manpower and financial aid.

In mid-March 2014 April accepted OM's invitation to discuss

this new vision with the mission's Africa area leaders. She spent her first and last weeks at the office in Pretoria, South Africa, and visited Kabwe, Zambia, during the four weeks in between. The conviction grew that she was on the right track. Leaders agreed that OM's training college in Kabwe would make a logical base for a new department that would reach into the whole Africa area, training and mobilizing churches to work with street children. The ministry would be called Hope on the Streets for Children.

April returned to the UK brimming with enthusiasm, eager to finalize her plans and share the mandate she'd received with churches and other contacts. She prayed that they too would want to get on board.

'It is not the responsibility of society to punish children and young people for what they have become in order to survive,' April passionately reasoned with all who invited her to speak. 'Society's responsibility is to punish those who have driven these young people to their condition, and to care for the victims. It breaks our hearts when these young people are demonized by society – even sometimes by the Church, which should be aiding them.

'The ministries we want to start will be sustainable within each country,' she explained, 'because if foreign money is required and this funding stops, then boys and girls are put back on the streets and further traumatized. I have seen ministries collapse and we have rescued children who were abandoned a second time. Our own ministry almost completely died when finances dried up after we had to leave the country. Homes were found for our boys, but this is rarely the case.

'God is a Father to the fatherless; therefore, He expects the Church to be a family to the fatherless. Our call is to serve as a good family. If we come alongside believers and community members, and equip and empower them with the necessary training, they will be able to run their own professional, godly and sustainable programmes.'

Keen to return to Zambia and begin assembling a core team, April intended to spend only a few weeks in the UK. However, the critical illness of a much-loved aunt altered her plans. Edna Holden had faithfully stood by her niece ever since she had taken her first step into missions. Now April felt privileged to remain available to her as much as possible, until the long fight with cancer was over. Later, she helped a cousin sort out the earthly belongings Edna had left behind.

April finally moved to Zambia under OM's auspices in July 2014. Even on her first visit she had been struck by the contrast of this country to the other parts of Africa where she'd lived. Zambia had officially proclaimed itself Christian. Bible verses hung boldly in the immigration office and Christian music played on buses. The atmosphere of religious freedom was refreshing.

Zambia was also more economically developed, and a greener place in which to live, especially during the rainy season. The majority of residents spoke English. Although April noticed similarities in manner and habits between the three African nations she'd lived in, Zambian society presented a curious mingling of African and Victorian English customs. Younger people curtsied to their elders, for instance, and used formal titles of address, such as Mr and Mrs or Aunt and Uncle, instead of first names. Perhaps this was a remnant of the long period its residents lived under British influence, when the nation went by the name of Northern Rhodesia.

April's new life in Kabwe, however, was very different from what she had experienced before. Here the challenge was more to adjust to the OM team's international culture rather than the local Zambian culture. She was glad to have a partially furnished home ready to move into when she arrived, with a living area, kitchen, toilet, shower and two bedrooms. The place was located in a secure housing complex on the outskirts of Kabwe. To reach the training base she could either catch a bus to town and then transfer to a shared taxi the rest of the way or else use the OM shuttle vehicle provided at the beginning and end of each working day.

Her first two months in a discipleship and orientation programme helped April make friends. Since the training of recruits to work with vulnerable children on the streets would not officially get underway until January 2015, she used the intervening months to do further research, prepare the curriculum and plan her strategy for the project. She also assisted in training teachers at OM's Bethesda School for disabled children. Although she was excited about the potential of her future ministry, her old enemy – self-doubt – crept in.

She prayed: 'Lord, I really don't want to pioneer again. I don't want to be a leader. I'm no good at it, and it's too hard . . .' After a while April realized that her adversary, the devil, was trying to turn her away from God's direction. She laid her insecurities at the Lord's feet and repented.

Melvin Chiombe – who was the Zambia field leader when she arrived and who later became the associate area leader, then the area leader of the whole Africa field – was her greatest mentor and encourager. He listened patiently as she went through the ups and downs of establishing the new work.

'I know you can do this,' Melvin would say, again and again. 'I have every confidence in you!'

Zambia's new field leader, Isaac Ngambi, and the whole OM Kabwe family also supported her. These brothers and sisters in Christ were faithful in providing gentle rebuke or encouragement when it was needed, and ensured that April didn't overtax her physical strength. She was grateful for their concern that God's work would progress His way, and that she was living up to all that she could be as His servant.

Back in the UK, April had come across an excellent training curriculum for professionals working with trauma and crisis in children. This material, written and/or compiled by Phyllis Kilbourn of WEC International, became the core of her training. WEC and other publishers generously gave her permission to print books in Africa, which made them more affordable to students. She also obtained 2,000 copies at a huge discount from Send the Light in the USA. Although she rearranged and added to the curriculum to suit the department's needs, the bulk of it remained Phyllis's work. April was extremely grateful for this invaluable resource.

April's first step in getting her new ministry up and running was preparing the people who would join her core team of facilitators. Zambians Gift Malambo and Austin Nyanwa, plus Anne Davidson from Scotland, were in her inaugural class. South African OM-er Ronel de Jong sat in for a month of the course to help her personal ministry, and Brazilian Nubia Goncalves, who was then heading up Mercy House in Kabwe, also participated. A Jamaican lady named Doris Fraser, who was with OM SportsLink and a psychologist by training, helped once a week with teaching. Austin had had some previous training in trauma, so although he was a student he also occasionally stepped in to teach when April had too many commitments. In her words they 'muddled through' by God's grace, and by that April she had a fledgling team composed of Anne, Austin and Gift (who served part of the time with another department until he became a full-time member). Doris joined them part time as well.

The Crisis Care Curriculum they used focused on healing the hurting hearts of children traumatized through war, sexual exploitation, loss of one or both parents from disease or other life-changing crises. Those on the course learned how they could be instrumental in shaping a more positive future for these children, and how important it was to care for their caregivers too. Part of these lessons came (with permission) from a programme designed by neuroscientist Dr Carolyn Leaf.

Of course, anyone serious about helping Africa's homeless children could not neglect the tragic consequences of the HIV and AIDS pandemic. During the years April worked in North Africa, the issue had seldom even been acknowledged by the government, and it was impossible to get her boys tested. Yet worldwide, of the estimated 3.2 million children under the age of 15 who currently live with the human immunodeficiency virus (HIV), approximately 91 per cent reside in Africa. Many young people are unaware that they have been infected. If the virus is left untreated, it can lead to acquired immune deficiency syndrome, better known as AIDS. AIDS takes the life of one out of six adolescents in this continent. It has also been responsible for turning millions of boys and girls into orphans, defined by the United Nations as children who have lost at least one parent. Of approximately 17 million under-17-year-olds who fit that description globally, a staggering 90 per cent live in Africa.

Fear is the greatest factor that drives HIV-positive or AIDS-orphaned children to the streets. Although the virus is only transmitted from person to person via blood, breast milk and sexual fluids, many are afraid they can 'catch' the disease simply by inhaling the breath of someone who is infected, drinking from the same cup or shaking a person's hand. HIV is popularly regarded as a curse and it is believed that if this curse remains in the house the whole family will suffer. So with no one willing to house them, rejected children are left to fend for themselves.

Even if a child isn't infected to start with, it is not possible to live on the streets for long without becoming highly vulnerable to viral infection through rape, drug use, sexual bartering or other intimacy. Often boys and girls don't have a safe place to spend their nights. Sex may be used as a way to secure protection and acceptance, especially for newcomers on the streets. In addition, substance abuse alters children's judgement and makes them vulnerable and more likely to contract or spread HIV via needles or sex. Without access to the health information, screening and treatment options available to the rest of society, it is no surprise that HIV prevalence among street children greatly exceeds that of the general child population.

AIDSLink Africa, one of the groups that April works with, focuses on restoring hope and dignity to people infected with and affected by HIV and AIDS. Its holistic strategy includes advocacy, prevention programmes, support groups, prayer initiatives and pre-natal care. AIDSLink challenges the attitude of the Church towards people living with HIV and AIDS; this includes children who end up orphaned or on the streets.

AIDSLink's Holly Keur described her encounter with one such child:

> The first time I saw Mary *(pseudonym)* she was curled into a ball from hunger pangs. The girl and her brother were orphaned by AIDS-related causes. Adding to their grief and fear was the fact that they were both HIV-positive. Their foster mother genuinely loved them but didn't have the resources to feed them properly because she had many other kids in her care. One day Mary didn't come home from school. It was finally discovered that this underage child was selling her body in the inner city. The girl was taken to a Christian safe house to work through the issues she faced on the street, but she ran away and went back to earn money as a sex worker. It was sad not only that Mary was hurting her own chances for a better future, but that every man she had a relationship with was also in danger of contracting HIV. And each of them could pass on the virus to others.

Holly's husband Nigel, also on the AIDSLink staff, admitted that as a child of only 11 he rebelled against his Christian upbringing and deliberately turned to life on the streets. Soon Nigel was using hard drugs, then dealing them and running with a gang. After he was arrested a few times he was considered an outcast by his community. Most people predicted that he would either end up in prison or die young. But then God in His mercy intervened. He took Nigel from the streets and a lifestyle that could have easily infected him with HIV, and restored him to the person he was meant to be. Today Nigel and Holly, through AIDSLink Africa, are part of a team committed to helping the marginalized, stigmatized and oppressed of society – especially those affected by HIV and AIDS. The child who was once without hope himself is now bringing hope to others.

April sees great advantages in a cooperation between Hope on the Streets for Children (HSC) and AIDSLink. In fact, some of her staff have been trained by AIDSLink. HSC uses some of AIDSLink's materials, and partners with them for occasional training of facilitators. April expects their two ministries will work together even more closely as more churches start projects that could use AIDSLink counsellors. She and her team are determined to offer more options to the tens of thousands of other 'Nigels' and 'Marys' who find themselves on a dead-end street.

12

The birth of a team

<hr>

And anyone who welcomes a little child like
this on my behalf is welcoming me.
(Words of Jesus, Matthew 18.5, NLT)

Looking back, April can see that her eagerness to get things done
has often resulted in pushing herself – and the people around her – a
little too hard.

> It has been said that one of my strengths is recognizing people's
> potential and mentoring/training them to achieve that. The negative
> side is that I sometimes try to rush them or rush ahead of God. I
> have found that a personal discipline of structured solitude and a
> daily walk with the Lord, plus one-on-one mentoring with each team
> member, helps me with this. Also, my own mentors help me to calm
> down – and slow down.
>
> When I first came to Zambia I was frustrated at how long it took
> to train people, because this delayed the start of the 'real' work. I
> just had to learn from my mistakes. In my previous country I was
> very close to my team but got too busy – after the first few years and
> opening the third centre – to spend the quality time I needed with
> them. I can safely say that I really only learned to be a good, rounded
> leader in Zambia – though I can still improve. I joke that I am a better
> trainer because I can train people not to make the same mistakes
> I did!

April's newly minted Hope on the Streets for Children facilitators
soon launched into spreading the vision, motivated to mobilize and
equip churches to set up their own pilot projects in their communities. The statistics spoke for themselves. Zambia had some 1.2
million orphans, according to UNICEF, and 20,000 children were

living or working on the streets. The team also arranged public discussion forums and spoke at pastors' fellowship meetings. These groups of Evangelical pastors from different churches in each region met once a week for prayer, so they offered an excellent platform for introducing the idea of helping children at risk.

In May 2015 April put the facilitators in charge of a second three-month class to train more facilitators. If the students had trouble understanding the various British, Scottish, Jamaican and Zambian accents of their teachers they didn't complain.

Yet generating momentum for the new ministry was not easy. People in the churches usually agreed with what they heard, and they said it was a wonderful vision. Then they would do nothing. But slowly individuals did get involved. The team established a Pastors' Fellowship Street Children's Committee, which got temporarily derailed due to various reasons, but has since been rescued and reformed.

To April's initial dismay, team member Austin Nyanwa was suddenly called back to his home church to become the regional coordinator for the Salvation Army. It was very hard for her to lose one of her main trainers, and Austin also headed up the facilitation work. She wondered what God was doing. But her star pupil went on to establish a very large street children's ministry programme in Lusaka with the Salvation Army, and God provided new leaders to replace him in Kabwe.

Austin explains how he got involved with April's project.

For some time I had had a love and interest in street children, and I shared this with the OM Zambia director. However, I had little information on how I could approach such children and minister to them. Then I met April Holden when she visited Zambia in 2013. She explained the passion and vision which God had given her, and though at the time she didn't say anything about my interest, I was later informed that April was happy with me and would like to work with me when she came back.

I prayed that she would return to Zambia, and God answered my prayer. Little did I know that she had gone home to organize funds to start her new training ministry!

There were five students in that first class. I was proud at first, thinking I knew everything, but by the end of the training I was transformed. The greatest impact that will remain with me for ever is how to love and reach street children, how to mobilize churches and set up a ministry for them. After we registered this course with the government we had a great breakthrough with invitations to train Zambian policemen, churches and NGOs; we became known to everyone in the community.

April and OM Zambia thought to enrol me as a team member, serving as the Zambia facilitator for church mobilization, a driver, and the one to handle departmental finances. Just as we were settling this, however, my church called me back to help with leadership development and church planting. It was difficult to leave and I struggled to be away from my leader, April. One thing she told me, however, was not to look backwards, but to be a light wherever I was. So I look at it that way and have shared the vision of transforming the lives of street children with the Salvation Army in Zambia.

And guess what the Lord has done! The Army agreed to support about 1,000 street children with a feeding programme that started in September 2017, and about 200 will be taken to learn at skill-training centres. For sustainability purposes we will fund the drop-in centre with a chicken raising project, so when the Salvation Army stops supporting them they will have a resource to depend upon.

I thank April for all she did for me and my small family. I was very sorry to leave her in 2015, but she remains an honour in my life. I benefited greatly from the street children training. One of my guiding verses is: 'Religion that God our Father accepts as pure and faultless is this: to look after orphans and widows in their distress and to keep oneself from being polluted by the world' (James 1.27).

Another loss to April's fledgling team came in January 2015, when Anne Davidson agreed to run the Mercy House project in Kabwe. April actually encouraged Anne to accept this position, as her skills were clearly needed to help Zambia's vulnerable children. Anne related:

The day I met April Holden I was into my fourth month of Missionary Discipleship Training in South Africa, a six-month course run by OM to prepare wannabe missionaries for the realities of mission life. When April came into the lecture hall, I thought, 'This is not the warrior woman I expected to see! I mean, if you are going to work with street kids God has to make you big and tough looking with a strong personality, right?' And here was this small lady with grey, wiry hair. She was softly spoken with a nice English accent.

April began to show some slides of life in North Africa and shared stories of the challenges she had faced. When she was finished she spoke of a new work she was going to pioneer in Zambia, a street kids' training school, and told us she needed workers to join her. Well, my heart started beating fast. Working with vulnerable children was my calling.

God told me that at that point I was at a junction on my walk with Him. I could carry on with my plan after discipleship training and volunteer at AIDS Hope, a vulnerable children's centre in Mamelodi township in South Africa, or I could make the decision to follow April to Zambia. The second choice was the hard road into the unknown, He said. It would be full of pain and obstacles, but I would grow a lot faster as a children's worker, and also grow closer to Him.

I decided there and then to see April after her talk and ask her if I could join the team. We had only a quick 15-minute chat, then prayed and exchanged emails. 'We shall see what God does. Keep praying,' she said, and off she went. I finished my six-month course and was accepted to go to OM Zambia in January 2015. I was so excited that finally, at the age of 38, God had decided to use me to help kids who were suffering.

I had some months to fill before going to Zambia and wanted to start applying what I'd learned, so I asked AIDS Hope if I could join them short term in Mamelodi. They agreed. I lived in a secure, walled compound with the other missionaries and had a nice bed and hot shower – then saw the reality of how some of the children in Africa live. Spending a few hours helping them with homework and playing with them each day didn't seem enough. I visited some of the kids' houses and fought back the tears. Tin shacks, with mud floors that in rainy season were wet, muddy and damp. It was very hot and dark as there was no ventilation or windows; the smell was unpleasant. It was hard to imagine how one father raised his four kids in the space of a small garden shed. How did they sleep at night? How could they cope with so little water (maybe five litres every three days for bathing, washing dishes and drinking)? This world is so unfair, Jesus, I thought. I hate it!

Many nights I lay awake asking God why He had to send

missionaries to help these kids when He could just come down and ease their sufferings Himself. I was just a big lassie who didn't have a clue what to do and I felt so helpless. I learned a lot in those few months, and the hopelessness I saw around me weighed heavily on my shoulders. We couldn't rescue them all and give them new houses and lives. It wasn't practical. So what was the answer?

When I finally arrived at the OM training base in Kabwe, Zambia, I felt exhausted. April came to visit me the next day. We chatted about her course and she gave me some books on street kids to look over. OM Zambia required me to do their discipleship training for two months, so at night I read the books and training module on traumatized children April had given me.

Finally the day came when I started April's training full time. I was so happy. The five of us in the class were her first-ever street kid students in Zambia. For the next two months I listened intently. What struck me most was realizing there were well-planned procedures to go through before anyone should even consider rescuing a street child. Others had gone before us and tested strategies so people like me could learn from their mistakes – and there were many of those. April openly shared her own failures with us. I soon understood that this was a job where I would mess up, but as I learned from the messes I would get better at street kid work.

I loved listening to April tell about how she got into some scary situations with some of the young lads who almost killed each other over small incidents. How that wee woman broke up fights between big street boys I'll never know. I was going to have to be brave, I decided.

After seeing the appalling, inhumane living conditions in Mamelodi I realized why children ran away from home (if that's what you could call it). April taught us how sexual abuse, the death of both parents, mistreatment from a step-parent, wars, neglect, extreme poverty and hunger were all contributing factors as to why a child ends up living on the streets. And when they get on the streets the abuse doesn't stop.

I remember one of our outreaches on the streets of Kabwe. A local pastor took us to where the street kids liked to hang out and gamble. We were to observe from a distance and see how they lived, without disturbing them. I was shocked as a man in a suit threw a glass bottle at the kids and insulted them in his language.

They were treated as if they were dogs! How were they ever going to get out of the street to a place of safety? They were so damaged. Did anyone care about these boys?

April and I have very different personalities. She's a driver and a visionary. She wants results. I'm laid back and I don't take life too seriously. I go with the flow. I wondered how partnering with her would work. But I knew God was the One behind our meeting.

As the weeks went on I could see April's passion and obsession for helping street kids all over Africa. She would not give up trying to mobilize the Church and local Christians to be God's answer to the overwhelming problem of children on the streets in Africa. I used to ask her, 'Can't we just set up a centre for street kids here in Kabwe and help them? The church here doesn't have money and they are not interested in being mobilized. They want us to do the work for them!'

'We are not here to work directly with the children,' April would remind me. 'We must train as many workers as we can and they will open the centres and be there for the children.'

She spoke again of her vision of a small river growing bigger and wider as it travelled, until it was a fast-flowing, giant waterway like the Zambezi River. 'We can't give up and just do a small thing here in Kabwe. God has bigger plans for Africa and His street children!'

I'm sure that's why God had me work with April. She stuck to the vision and I learned so much about empowering others instead of trying to do it all myself. She taught me how well-intentioned missionaries can mess things up if they don't involve the local people. Community participation is key to any project's success, as the people will then own it as their own – not see it as a foreigner's project, because they have given the money. I really believe April's course challenged my thinking as to how to handle the huge homeless problem.

When we finished the training, we discovered that most of us from that first-ever class were expected to become the next teachers of the street children's curriculum.

'No way, April. I'm not a teacher!' I objected, adding that I'd be much too nervous. 'I've just learned this stuff theoretically. I've no practical work or experience with street boys. How am I going to teach?'

Well, she wasn't about to listen to my concerns and insisted I would do fine. She would be in class to observe me. All I needed was practice and a confidence boost.

I thought being a lecturer on a subject I'd just learned was the toughest thing God had ever challenged me with, but April was a good mentor/leader; she could see people's gifts and encourage them to do things they never thought they could achieve. She just wouldn't take no for an answer. God was right to send me to April! I was pushed to do things I was previously too fearful to try, and matured as a result.

One year on with street kids' education in Zambia, and God saw that I was ready for an even bigger challenge. The Mercy House project for vulnerable children had been started in Kabwe by an OM-er named Nubia Goncalves some years before. Now she was going back home to Brazil and looking for a replacement. April hinted that maybe I should step in. She knew I had learned a lot and that I was itching to personally help children in need. She even sent me to help Nubia, so I could get three months of hands-on experience with the project.

I refused to be the new leader, however. Leadership was tough and I wasn't anxious to take on a role like that. I worried that I would not be strong enough to run Mercy House, which was in the second biggest shanty town in sub-Saharan Africa.

But as God often did, He spoke to me one day through one of the vulnerable children. David *(not his real name)* was hanging about, hugging me and looking for attention. I knew he had a dad and a stepmom, but he was well known in Makalulu compound as the kid who wasn't loved. He often got into trouble and found someone to fight with.

Mercy House was still at the building stage, almost ready to re-open as a boys' day care centre with classes and teachers and a cook. David came every day in the hope of getting some food, since he knew the staff would be there working. On this particular day he took my hands and laid them on his chest and I could feel his bones and his heartbeat. It was then I felt the world stop. All other distractions around me disappeared. It was as if God had stopped time and silenced the world. Then I heard Him speak.

'Anne, do you feel this wee heartbeat?'

'Yes, Lord, I feel it,' I replied.

'This heartbeat belongs to Me and it is very precious. I want you to look after this wee heart, and all the others that I give to you.'

I knew I could not say no. I saw how valuable those kids were, and if no one tried to help them they might end up on the streets. So I prayed hard and told God that I needed three confirmations, so I would know for sure I was in His will.

God gave me those confirmations and April was among those who gave me her blessing. It must have been hard for her. I had followed her to Zambia and she had trained me well. We made a good team, had learned how to work with each other, and I knew she wanted me to travel with her and train people all over Africa. But I really needed to learn how to run a project to gain practical experience. What use was I as a teacher for street kids' ministries if I myself had never worked with kids?

So in January 2015 I became the coordinator of Mercy House in Makalulu compound. In this area of Kabwe, Zambia, there are about 100,000 people living in poverty. A large percentage of the country's street kids are from Makalulu. Many are orphans or at risk because their parents don't look after them. AIDS has claimed the lives of some of these kids' parents, and the children are traumatized because they have been neglected and left with family that don't really want them. Extra kids are a burden to most families; they are more mouths to feed and bodies to clothe. These kids are lucky to have one meal a day and are used as an extra pair of hands to work about the house and do chores.

Many adult Zambian friends have told me of the mistreatment they went through as children because their mother or father remarried and the new parent rejected them. They didn't receive schooling, as it cost too much. They had no feeling of self-worth.

Many children live with an aunt or grandparent who struggles to meet their basic needs. Some children are terrified of their alcoholic parents, who turn to drink to cope with their hopelessness and take out their frustrations on their children or each other. Some kids from Makalulu can be found walking the 159-km road from Kabwe to Lusaka, Zambia's capital, because they cannot bear the situation at home and are going in search of their mothers. They have been left with aunts or relatives who mistreat them while their mother has gone to Lusaka to make money to send home to the family. These kids are desperate and will end up on the streets.

Life for an unloved, forgotten child in Makalulu is hellish. We want to break that cycle in their lives. Mercy House identifies the most vulnerable children and works with their families to improve each child's life. Once a child comes to Mercy House we make sure that they receive two meals daily: a snack and a hot, nutritious meal.

Each child gets one hour of basic education in a school-like environment and one hour of spiritual nurturing. We pray that they will learn they are much-loved children of God. We teach them boundaries and morals and prepare them to go to school. Some of them are too wild or too traumatized for school, so we offer counselling. We work with some of the parents and try to teach them how to look after their children. With the help of the Tabitha Initiative[6] we also offer a women's empowerment programme – business training and classes in tailoring – in the hope they can support their families a little better.

After the children have been with us for one year we can send them to a local school on a scholarship, but they attend our Saturday club to stay connected with us. We currently have about 100 children we try to help.

I always remember April saying, 'Let the community be involved in your project and it will be a success. Don't let it rely on your skills or depend on your finances. Set up projects that are locally sustainable so that if the foreigners have to leave the country it will keep going under the direction of the national people you have trained.'

She also taught me the power of using local men and women to teach their own communities. Africans often brush off the advice of Westerners, as if it doesn't apply to them, but they will listen to their buddies. So we train Zambians to serve as staff at the centre and in the community, to keep more children from going on the streets. An HIV and AIDS prevention and advice programme is run at the day centre by AIDSLink.

Soon, we will open a rescue and rehabilitation home for girls. April works very closely with me and she is on the advisory board for the new home. We decided on a partnership so she can send us interns and new team members and offer training for our people. She also helps us network with other groups.

I often wonder where I would be today if God hadn't sent April to my class that day in South Africa. What a big mess I would have made of Mercy House if I had not done her training! No doubt I would be a typical, thoughtless do-gooder, acting on emotion rather than as a trained disciple. April's course certainly knocked the naivety out of me!

After Anne left to take up her new responsibility, God was faithful in supplying a vital reinforcement for April's depleted team. Laura Jenkins, her friend and fellow teacher in two previous African countries, had returned to the USA several years before and begun teaching at a Christian school. When April wrote to urge Laura to help set up the new street children's ministry in Zambia, she sought God's will in the matter and agreed. Although she was delayed by her struggle to raise support at home in the USA, she made it to the field by the end of 2015.

'I love teaching,' Laura explained, 'and to be teaching others how to handle traumatized street children is a bonus. I consider that April and I are just duplicating ourselves so that more children may be helped to get off the streets and into permanent, stable places to live. There are more people in churches in Africa than there are children on the streets. If the Church were fully involved, the problems and troubles of the children on the streets would be resolved. I am helping to alleviate this problem. I know God has called me to this ministry and this valuable work.'

April was deeply thankful for Laura's friendship and expertise. God had sent exactly the right partner at the right time to face the challenges appearing on the horizon.

13

Compassion without borders

Enlarge the place of your tent, stretch your tent curtains wide,
do not hold back; lengthen your cords, strengthen your stakes.
(Isaiah 54.2)

Despite all the ups and downs, sickness and struggles, praises and questioning, the Lord patiently established His vision for Hope on the Streets for Children. The programme had five facets, with a different team member appointed to lead each of them: prevention, facilitation, networking/prayer, training and administration.

When April realized that her students would profit by practising the theory they learned in the classroom, she contacted Nsansa. This well-established ministry was not part of OM, but it was run by former OM Zambian Jasper Mutale and his Japanese wife, Zion. Nsansa had been operating for about a dozen years in Zambia's capital, Lusaka. Besides opening a street church it had built a children's village that included a school for orphans. Nsansa also did community work with the families of children on the street. The project was mostly funded from within Zambia and Jasper generated income by writing newspaper articles, and running a music business and other enterprises.

Hope on the Streets for Children formed a partnership with Nsansa and began sending students as interns. Jasper had developed an excellent programme, but it was growing almost too rapidly; he needed help to fine-tune the operation. So the arrangement benefited both parties: HSC's training of Nsansa staff raised that ministry's standards. It also networked with them and assisted with fundraising. In later years, four of the HSC team helped to develop a halfway house for Nsansa. April was glad to have a model available where facilitators-in-training and new team members could gain valuable, hands-on experience.

April could see that many of her students were being impacted by the urgency of outreach to vulnerable children. At the same time the training helped them understand how hurts in their own past had affected them, and how they could deal with them.

'I have found healing from my own traumas so I can help others,' affirmed one trainee.

'I didn't realize the needs street children had,' someone else admitted. 'I thought we could just feed them and put them in school. Now I understand they need full support and love, and their foundational needs restored.'

April rejoiced when students told her, 'One week of training has been like one year to me, because it has impacted my life so much.' And: 'I didn't think I could do this work, but now look at me!'

She was aware, however, that effective action on behalf of Africa's vulnerable children had to go beyond the reach of church and mission workers. The cooperation of community social service staff was equally essential. Young people who lived on the streets were commonly ignored, scorned and abused across the continent – across the world, really – even by civil authorities whose duty it was to protect them.

Uganda was one of the worst offenders. With an estimated 2.7 million orphans, this country had perhaps the most notorious record of police brutality. The Human Rights Watch, an independent group that spotlights abuses worldwide, interviewed dozens of homeless Ugandan children who were routinely threatened, harassed, robbed and beaten with sticks by police. Some officers had damaged the children's ankles to the point where they could no longer walk properly.

April was determined to pursue every possible avenue to work with the police, social workers and prison officers. After Hope on the Streets offered a training course to 45 police officers in Zambia, their evaluations included revelations such as this: 'I don't slap street children now. I really understand them'; 'I feel better able to help the children who come to us'; 'This training has changed my life'; 'I spend time with my own children now and really try to be there for them'; 'The training has helped me understand the children coming to us'; 'I've been helped even with understanding my own family'; 'We have learned to be more spiritual'.

A chaplain on the force reported that they no longer received complaints from the public about how officers abused children. This needed to happen on a wider scale.

In 2016 April extended the reach of HSC's ministry by introducing distance learning. Initially six students travelled to Kabwe from North Africa and within Zambia, joining a seventh student from Holland who was already there. Their focus for the next three weeks was the topic of 'Trauma and Crisis Care and Transitional Care Models for Street Children'. The two men serving in North Africa ran a programme among street children and had to cope with particularly difficult circumstances. They wanted to start a course in car mechanics for the young men. All of the class members were committed to learning all they could, thoroughly engaging in the issues that were discussed. When they returned to their home countries they continued studying, carrying out practical assignments and maintaining regular contact through email.

One participant explained how the training permanently reconfigured his attitude:

Before July 2016 my life was very different than it is today. I was another person and a bad father; my children feared me a lot. I beat them when they did wrong things or if they made a lot of noise, cried or played in the sand. When I got angry they would panic. I didn't know what to do.

But coming home after doing the Hope for Children on the Streets training my life was transformed. I learned a lot of things that helped me to better understand how to deal with children and what their basic needs are. I learned that a child doesn't need only food and health care and shelter – he or she needs your love, time and attention. Doing things like playing with sand, making noise and crying is a part of their life and they can't do without it. Before the training I did not know about this.

In my culture we beat children to educate them, because we think if you don't beat children when they are young they'll not listen to you when they become big. They may even beat you, because they don't have respect for you.

Now, if you saw me playing with my children, you would be

surprised. My parents, my wife and friends are all amazed by my transformation. I have now become a friend to my children. They trust me and want always to be around me, playing. If their mother yells at them they run to me!

The way I treat the street kids has also changed, because I now know that each and every one of them has his own story; I also understand why they take drugs. When people say bad things about street children I always explain that they are wrong. 'Just put yourself in his place,' I say. 'If it were you, you would do the same. Don't think they are happy to be doing what they do.'

HSC welcomed opportunities to network with all relevant ministries in Zambia. One team member invested time in Bethel Chapel, a Kabwe church that had started a day centre for children after catching the vision. Abba's Heart was another programme for orphans and other kids on the streets already established in Kitwe, the country's second largest city. When a new three-month training course started for four additional students in June 2017, two women represented Abba's Heart. They were preparing for involvement in a new rescue and rehabilitation home for street girls.

In 2017, Hope on the Streets for Children split into two teams. April and Laura maintained overall responsibility for the whole HSC Africa area team as travelling trainers and consultants. As they coordinated, mentored and connected the facilitators in various countries, they explored possibilities for opening new branches. The two women had so far trained people in Ghana, Zambia, Zimbabwe, Mozambique and the Lake Tanganyika area. When they were back in Zambia they continued to participate in training facilitators at the OM base, and mentoring the newly appointed HSC Zambia leaders, Alex and Janet Mulenga.

Alex and Janet both had solid theological training, as well as experience in working with churches and schools through Scripture Union. Most importantly they had a passion to serve vulnerable children. The Mulengas' team included eight Zambians plus a female social worker from the Netherlands. Other individuals assisted with teaching, particularly an experienced South African counsellor named Karin Menkveld, who was with OM's teacher training programme. Karin decided to join HSC in January 2018, overseeing internship students while continuing her counselling work on the compound. The HSC Zambia team ran training workshops at the Kabwe churches and other congregations besides networking with various ministries that already existed for children at risk.

Laura was assisting Alex and OM Zambia field leader Isaac as they applied to government bodies to get the HSC curriculum accredited in that country. Accreditation would make an important difference, giving HSC students a qualification in psychosocial counselling to use within the community. It meant they could help traumatized children or school kids without fear of breaking the law.

With roots firmly established in Zambia, Hope on the Streets for Children was already spreading into other African countries in critical need of that hope.

14

Invisible children

If anyone causes one of these little ones – those who believe in
me – to stumble, it would be better for them if a large millstone
were hung around their neck and they were thrown into the sea.

(Mark 9.42)

Zambia: Lake Tanganyika

In August 2015, April took the HSC team to Mpulungu, Zambia's
only port on Lake Tanganyika. They had been given a bus for travelling and training, and the fact that it was adapted for people with
disabilities allowed Gift Malambo to join the team for the long 12-
hour journey.

Gift was in charge of the ministry's networking and prayer, and
he had done an excellent job in linking both new and existing programmes together with individuals who had the vision. His goal was
to provide ideas as to how to interface with business people, government bodies and other stakeholders who could assist with tackling
the work among children on the street, and create projects sustainable within Zambia.

Gift had been injured many years before in a bus accident on
his way home from Lake Tanganyika, where he used to work. His
legs were left paralysed and he had only partial use of his hands.
He hadn't been back since his accident, so he was both excited and
nervous about travelling back to the lake with his wife, and facing
his memories. Besides offering two weeks of training to 25 OM-ers
working with orphans and other children at risk, April intended the
trip to serve as a team-building exercise.

Africa's Lake Tanganyika is the longest freshwater lake in the world, and the second deepest. The people who live along the shores are heavily reliant on fishing to make a living. For this reason families tended to be large, averaging seven to nine children. By the age of seven, most boys are capable of helping with the fishing. Daughters can be married off at the age of 12 or 14, often to old men who already have many wives, in order to bring added income to parents from sons-in-law. It is not unusual for men to abuse or divorce their wives after they've had a few children. As a result, people living around Lake Tanganyika don't see the value or need of education. In some villages, no one has ever finished school in their 100-year history.

The traditional belief that spirits are involved in all activities is deeply rooted. To people's way of thinking, a poor catch of fish indicates a spiritual problem. In order to solve that problem the spirits need to be pleased or appeased, and this might mean sacrificing their children. Parents with this world view see their offspring as tools to be used for money. This is why they invest little emotional care in their children. It is rare to see parents showing a deep attachment to sons and daughters. On the other hand, children also distance themselves from family members, because they sense where they stand. Some don't even know the names of their parents.

In recent years, climate change and overfishing have led to smaller catches of fish. This has made children even more vulnerable. With little to do apart from fishing, both children and adults often take up drinking and smoking. Serious poverty, disease, illiteracy and social problems have resulted in abnormally high death rates and an increasing population of orphans. Although 'leftover' children usually have relatives, no one really looks after their welfare. They are the outcasts, treated as slaves or servants, with little hope of receiving an education.

At the time of the HSC team visit, no less than 46 per cent of Mpulungu's 130,000 residents were children under 15. Many of them were either orphans or physically vulnerable in some way. The high incidence of the AIDS virus in the region had left the community devastated. Although schooling was free for orphans up to the age of 12 or 13 at government schools in Zambia, educational standards and conditions were poor.

About ten years ago, OM began to offer an education to 40

neglected 5- and 6-year-olds. Today over 180 students attend the Good News II school up to the age of 12, receiving two daily meals, a school uniform and other educational supplies. OM also sponsors children older than this, who have continued on to government schools. This includes helping with school books, uniforms and fees.

'Here at the Good News II school, we want to help keep the girls from early marriages and the boys from going astray,' affirmed Christopher Kasale, OM Lake Tanganyika's field leader. 'Our mission is to care physically, emotionally and spiritually for the orphans and other at-risk children in Mpulungu. By providing a Christ-centred education and ensuring good parental care, we want to guide them into a close relationship with Jesus.'

Christopher agreed that the training offered by Hope on the Streets for Children has had a great impact on their ministry. OM workers are able to help guardians and teachers know how to take better care of boys and girls with difficult backgrounds. This closes the gap between the parents and children. With practical tips and project management training, many start to look for different ways to provide for their families, apart from fishing. Communities are also involved in this process. As the concept of caring for the next generation starts to sink in, it is bound to bring about great improvement in Lake Tanganyika society.

Headteacher Laban Chipili, the first local man ever to receive teacher training, enthused that the concept was eye-opening for the teachers. He explained that since receiving instruction from HSC facilitators, staff were able to identify what was really going on with their students. The trauma suffered by most of them had triggered negative behaviour, such as fighting. In the past, teachers would punish the children without dealing with the root cause. Now, with the understanding gained from Hope on the Streets training, teachers sat down with 'problem kids' to learn the real issues. Then their guardians were invited to the school to discuss the situation. By gently gaining more information about the childrens' background and what happened in the past, the teachers could handle them more compassionately.

'Many guardians, as well, had no clue as to why their children behaved as they did,' said Laban. 'After talking it over with teachers, they too realize what is troubling the boys and girls. With better care from adults around them, the young ones also start to open up.'

Laban described the case of one nine-year-old student who always dozed off during classes. The teacher used to just wake the little girl and ask her to move around to keep her more alert. 'We thought that she didn't have enough food or sleep, but that was not the real reason,' he shared. The teachers decided to consult with her guardians for more insight. As they delved deeper into the child's background they found out it was probable that her father, when he was still alive, had taken her to the witch doctor. In exchange for some supposed gain for himself he may have performed witchcraft rituals intended to give evil powers the rights to his daughter's spirit. Since her father was her authority in the spirit realm, this would naturally have a powerful influence on her well-being and development. After learning the story, one of the teachers tried to pray for the girl. She immediately fell down and manifested great agitation. Finally, they were able to deal with her inner issue and cast out the evil that was controlling her spirit. Because of her father's actions this little girl had been a captive, but she was now set free.

The shores of Lake Tanganyika are not the only areas in Africa where child sacrifice is still practised. The charity KidsRights believes hundreds of children have been murdered in recent years by a network of witch doctors who have turned human sacrifice into a lucrative business. A child's purity and innocence is supposed to make the sacrifice all the more potent. Other vulnerable people, however, such as those with disabilities, albinos and women, have been hunted, mutilated and killed for this purpose. A *Human Rights Brief* (Salisbury, 2012) cites reports of this activity coming from Nigeria, Uganda, Swaziland, Liberia, Botswana, South Africa, Tanzania, Namibia and Zimbabwe. Because of the secrecy involved, the majority of these incidents go unreported and uninvestigated.

April is deeply thankful that the HSC training has equipped OM's Lake Tanganyika team to be much more sensitive in assisting disadvantaged children. Instead of imposing rules and labels on their students, teachers have learned first of all to listen to their stories, recognizing that each of them will need special care in order to experience God's healing.

'The children here have tough lives. I am really grateful for the training,' summarized Laban. 'Now I know better how to help children with trauma.'

Ghana: carrying too heavy a burden

Among the world's forgotten children are the thousands of boys and girls who are trafficked from Ghana's less-developed northern villages to provide cheap labour in the south. Many of these young ones are used for the fishing industry on Lake Volta, one of the world's largest artificial lakes. Sometimes they are required to dive to disentangle fish nets from the numerous tree stumps under the water. This dangerous job can lead to infection from water-borne diseases or even drowning. Other young people are exploited as domestic servants or street vendors or forced into the sex trade.

'Since 2007 we've worked on education and prevention, giving talks in schools and urging community leaders to oppose such practices,' notes OM Ghana's field leader Christopher Insaidoo. 'Some parents willingly let their kids go, but don't understand what will happen to them. Other children are abused at home or their friends urge them to leave. When they don't want to go back home we have to find ways they can go to school or provide skilled training so they can safely bring in some income.'

Several years ago OM began targeting out-of-school teenage *Kayeye* girls living in the slums.[7] *Kayayie* or *kayeye* is a slang term meaning 'going to carry', applied to the countless boys and girls who work in the market places of South Ghana. These young people are 'head' porters, transporting everything from heavy loads of fruit, wood and bags of rice to tyres or other car parts on their heads. Some of the children or teenagers are trafficked from the more indigent north. Others leave home voluntarily, lured by a dream of earning big money for themselves or their families.

According to Portia Amoateng, who is in charge of OM Ghana's outreach to the Kayeye girls, factors that push children to the south include conflict, drought, famine, extreme religious activity, a poor economy and lack of job opportunities. Race and discrimination may also be involved, as well as political and social intolerance of any who question the status quo regarding, for instance, forced marriages.

An estimated 3,000 or more Kayeye live in the city of Kumasi alone. Most of the children gravitate to slum areas and often wind up begging on the streets, without adequate shelter and vulnerable to rape, robbery and other violence. If they do find a place to bed down it's likely to be a 3-metre square room without ventilation, shared with 10 to 15 others. Because these young people often can't afford to pay the fee required each time they want to visit the latrine or use the washroom to shower, constant exposure to germs leads to a high incidence of skin diseases. Poor nutrition adds to their fragile health.

Portia says that those who are able to find work in markets, farms and homes as domestic helpers are also subject to abuse by their employers – people who pretend to protect them. The majority of young girls are raped and forced into prostitution by their circumstances or through flesh-peddlers. The Kayeye are virtual slaves, without anyone to defend their rights.

OM's goal is to meet both their physical and spiritual needs, partnering with churches for the girls' healing and restoration. This involves raising awareness and setting up counselling centres, health and first aid services and practising friendship evangelism.

This was exactly the type of action that the Hope on the Streets for Children in Africa team wanted to encourage. OM Ghana gladly accepted April's offer to network, and in November 2016 Laura Jenkins and Marja Huisman travelled to Kumasi to train national workers.

Reports Portia:

OM Ghana children's ministry coordinator Ruthina Aryeete and I were privileged to be part of that first training in trauma and crisis for street children, levels one and two. It was very enlightening. We trainees were made aware of faulty behaviour we were already engaged in with the girls, like some of the gestures and physical touch we used and things we said. I hadn't known that these things could have a great negative impact on my relationship with street children, and my work.

I better understood through this training that vulnerable children like these are very sensitive, and social workers have to be smart and relational. I was equipped with key ethics behind initial relationship-building, trust-building and communication strategies as a social worker. May God bless Laura Jenkins and Marja Huisman for that knowledge.

The Ghana team continues to pursue distance learning, and HSC will conduct periodic training on site with the aim of establishing a permanent branch early in 2019. April is also committed to recruiting people to reinforce this crucial outreach.

Zimbabwe: the Church awakes

In March 2017, Laura and April travelled to Zimbabwe at the invitation of Eternal Word Ministries in Harare, to conduct nine days of training. One of OM's team members belonged to this major denomination which had almost 600 churches in Zimbabwe, and was already very active in working with orphans and other marginalized people. The goal of the HSC training was to facilitate the churches' mercy ministry as well as that of the OM team.

Zimbabwe needed all the help it could get. Years of political repression, high unemployment and massive food shortages caused by drought had led to destitution for 72 per cent of the population. Malnutrition and disease were rampant. A very large number of people lived with AIDS. Although the prevalence rate was declining through stepped-up prevention, screening and treatment strategies, some 1.6 million children had been orphaned through this disease alone. Another 40,000 died each year from infection.

April recalled:

We were very excited to meet the believers in Zimbabwe. They were so keen on the training! On the first Sunday Laura and I spoke at two different churches about the vision of becoming families to street children. That Monday and Tuesday we trained members of one congregation, then repeated the lessons on Wednesday and Thursday at the other church. All the students came together on Friday and Saturday at the main city church. On the final Sunday we spoke at a different place. In total we had 36 students and even before we left they had put together a plan of action for preventing children from going to the streets! They want us to go back and do more training.

One of the students confessed, 'Before this, I just pushed street children away and saw them as a nuisance. Now I see them as precious, traumatized children who need God.'

Another woman, after learning of the foundational needs of children and problems that cause trauma, promised, 'I will no longer abuse my children.' This was very brave for her to say in front of everyone, especially in an honour/shame culture such as that of Zimbabwe.

Crisis in Mozambique

That same spring April and Laura ran a training course in Mozambique, which lies alongside the Indian Ocean in the south of Africa. Although this country has been blessed with many natural resources, that bounty has been seriously depleted over the years by disastrous floods, droughts and 15 years of civil war. The resulting loss of livelihoods has put over half of Mozambique's 25-plus million people below the poverty line. Most can only expect to live an average of 58 years. The AIDS death rate is the fourth highest in the world, and millions of other men, women and children are subject to repeated attacks of malaria, cholera and numerous types of infectious diseases.

Laura and April were told that 45 per cent of Mozambique's population were under the age of 15. Those who were more fortunate enjoyed nine or ten years of schooling; the rest dropped out because they couldn't pay for school uniforms or books. These boys and girls had to work to help their families survive or else they would all end up on the streets.

Laura reported, 'We spent three weeks training 29 students at the OM base in Mocuba, the only missions training school in Mozambique. The base has ten hectares of land with several buildings, all in need of repair. The students were very passionate and diligent, but spoke only Portuguese, so we worked with translators. It was a wonderful experience. The training on trauma and trauma intervention impacted the people personally, as they have suffered much due to war and civil unrest. They had also developed a strong passion to rescue the children on the street and to work with

Invisible children

communities to prevent more children going to the streets. They are desperate for more training.'

Saddened by the overwhelming crisis in that country, April and Laura immediately began to raise funds for two of their Zambian team members to move to Mozambique. Sharon Kunda had raised six sons and daughters of her own; now God had given her a determination to help children without hope. Ephraim Zulu also had a servant's heart and was excited about following Jesus' call to Mozambique. Not only would this pair continue training workers, they would establish a permanent base in the city of Mocuba for Hope on the Streets for Children. They had already begun to prepare by studying Portuguese.

Madagascar: island paradise?

HSC Africa attempted to spread outside continental Africa to the island nation of Madagascar in 2017. Leading the effort was 20-year-old Englishwoman Deborah James. She explained:

> I joined Operation Mobilisation because I felt God was calling me to serve Him on the mission field. My passion is working with children: making sure that no child, regardless of circumstances, is ignored by the Church. So in May 2017 I travelled to Zambia, becoming part of Hope on the Streets for Children. I completed the training with the idea of starting an HSC department in Madagascar.
>
> The course was very helpful, and without it I think I would be lost in Madagascar. The teachers always had our best interests at heart, wanting to see us grow and develop into people with a heart and passion to help vulnerable children. They worked to give us knowledge and understanding of the challenges these children face and the difficulties we would face when working with them. I found that the course helped me to understand the background of children who end up living on the streets, and this helps me to be more aware and understanding when I meet them. I also found it very helpful to learn how to start a self-reliant project and the process that needs to occur to make it effective and sustainable for the lives of the children it will be impacting. I believe the course helped me to mature and prepare for the job that was ahead of me in the field. I am grateful to the team for nurturing and guiding me throughout those three months.

Madagascar is often presented to tourists as a tropical paradise. To others it has become known as the setting for a blockbuster movie featuring talking animals. However, the reality of life on this fourth-largest island in the world, located in the Indian Ocean off south-east Africa, is very different. Madagascar is on the United Nations top-25 list of least developed countries. Almost 45 per cent of its population of 25 million are children aged 14 or younger. Because of the country's economic problems, life is far from easy for these children and 82 per cent of those who are under 18 live below the poverty line. According to the World Bank, one in four between the ages of 5 and 17 have to work to support their families. Some may have jobs in mines or vanilla plantations. Others are sent to the city for domestic servitude or fall victim to the booming sex industry. According to the UN, a quarter of these children are subjected to severe health risks.

In 2013 the UN denounced the widespread sexual exploitation of children in Madagascar. Local communities and even parents regularly turn a blind eye to what has become a popular source of income. The child sex industry has led to an alarming increase in the number of children being trafficked to countries in the Middle East, according to the international Committee on the Rights of the Child.

The island also faces the consequences of natural disasters. Madagascar is one of the six countries most vulnerable to climate change and it has been ravaged by cyclones, droughts and locust invasions. These add to the hardships faced by a low-income population. As crops are destroyed, people can't afford to buy the basic foods needed for a nutritional diet. Malnutrition takes over, with 50 per cent of children below the age of five suffering from endemic and chronic malnutrition, otherwise known as stunting. Research shows that if a child is stunted by the age of two the damage to their young minds and bodies is virtually irreversible and will lead to other complications. In addition, infants are abandoned because mothers don't see any hope when they can't even feed their other children. In rural areas, girls in particular may be married off as young as ten because their families can't provide for them. Only 66 per cent of children finish primary school because they are often too hungry to concentrate or they are sent out to work.

More than a quarter of females in Madagascar become pregnant between the ages of 15 and 19. According to UNICEF, this has led to a quarter of children not getting registered at birth, leaving them more vulnerable to abuse and more likely to be excluded from social activities. In Madagascar, you have to provide a birth certificate to enter school.

There is no accurate data as to how many children live on the streets, but the number is estimated to be in the high thousands. The problem is not just boys and girls running away to live on the streets, but whole families who are being forced out of their homes due to Madagascar's economic problems. According to the Committee on the Rights of the Child, an alarming 1,000 or more children disappear each year in the capital city of Antananarivo. These lost ones most likely leave home because they are beaten by family members or else they are among the island's 900,000 orphans. Many end up living on the streets.

To some observers, the people of this country might seem to be caught in a hopeless spiral of poverty and disasters. However, when we look at them through God's eyes, we can see children who are in need of love and a personal identity or families who only require a helping hand so that they have the means to support themselves.

My vision for Madagascar is to proclaim the hope that Jesus gives us, and change the life of one child at a time until we start to see whole communities change. I want to share with the Church the mandate that God gave us and teach about the foundational needs and rights of a child. That is the first step. Then we can train people in the hope they will partner with us or set up their own ministry, such as a feeding programme or day centre. Once believers arise and take ownership of reaching those around them, they will be able to take God's love, hope and joy to the island's children – whether they are living on the streets of the capital or suffering from sexual abuse and malnutrition in rural townships. My goal is to empower the Church, because I know God can have a much bigger impact on this country through His Church than He can through me as an individual.

OM Madagascar's country leader, Hanitra Andrianomanana, had high hopes for this new endeavour on her island.

Having children is a very big thing here, but then parents can't really look after their children. They can't meet their needs. Only 60 out of 100 boys and girls complete their primary education, and this is because of poverty. I think most of the street children in Madagascar are not orphans. They have a family, but this family waits for their child to get something from other people and bring it back to them. Usually it is these children who are providing for their families.

Although churches in the city have a children's ministry, it is not focused on reaching out to those who are living on the streets. Most of the reason why people aren't already reaching out to these vulnerable children is that they haven't been challenged to do this. To meet the needs of street children you need hands and funds. I want to see Hope on the Streets for Children train the Church and others in Madagascar in order to help facilitate this work. HSC will inspire and equip people to reach out to the street children living in their communities. For those who are already involved in such work, the training will help them do it in a better way.

In 2018 Deborah and the OM Madagascar team had to face the fact that churches were not ready to work very much with even their own children. The team therefore decided to spend a year building up children's ministries within the Church. Deborah would head up this effort. After learning to value the spiritual and practical education of their own families they could then be equipped to address the needs of other children. If a re-evaluation at the end of that year proved that churches were ready to reach street children, HSC would recruit team members for Madagascar.

One of April's ongoing frustrations is finding partners to stand behind trained African missionaries. She knows scores of committed men and women who are ready and eager to serve with OM and Hope on the Streets teams. Often these Africans are most effective in impacting their own people, but they are prevented from entering the ministry by the shortage of minimal resources necessary to care for their families.

Lake Tanganyika (Zambia), Ghana, Zimbabwe, Mozambique, Madagascar: Hope on the Streets had made its first forays into a continent full of 'invisible children'. Not a big start, perhaps – but it was a beginning.

15

Back to the future

———•◦•———

Having heard all of this you may choose to look the other way – but you can never again say you did not know.
(William Wilberforce)

In 2017 April Holden agreed to head up an Africa Area Strategic Planning Task Force for OM Africa. The mandate of the group was to ask critical questions and formulate ideas for reaching out to the continent's least-reached people. Participants would also collect information by means of a SWOT (strengths, weaknesses, opportunities and threats) analysis of the mission's existing work as carried out by various ministry heads.

Although leading the task force would add to her already full workload, April saw this as a not-to-be-missed opportunity. The group's findings could give fresh impetus to the mission. Hopefully they would also affirm the role played by Hope on the Streets for Children.

The vision for HSC was already gaining momentum. In two years it had grown from just one person to 15, and from a single base in Zambia to exciting pioneering initiatives in Madagascar and Mozambique, as well as a sensitive, restricted-access nation in the north of the continent. In addition, the team had trained 158 students in five fields across Africa. Many of these graduates had proceeded to train other workers involved in various ministries and churches. Relationships between individuals and within families had been dramatically altered; countless children had been offered the prospect of a brighter future.

April tried to put her goals for the next five years on paper. Although her dreams often outran practicalities, she thought she could reasonably expect to achieve eight goals:

- strengthen HSC Zambia, Mozambique and Madagascar, and initiatives within North Africa;
- encourage the acceleration of church participation, equipping each group with appropriate guidelines and training;
- get more HSC-trained people into North Africa and Ghana;
- start two more HSC branches in Zimbabwe and Ghana;
- network internationally with other people in OM who work with or on behalf of vulnerable children and young people;
- travel and train outside the Africa area;
- continue following up former students to ensure effective application of training;
- network with other organizations in Africa that help children on the streets.

Within ten years, she hoped the ministry would be able to claim further territory, to have:

- offered some HSC training in all Africa area fields;
- placed several HSC trainers outside the Africa area;
- ensured all Africa area programmes that work with vulnerable children or young people include at least one person with trauma training;
- continued sending and basing HSC trainers in different fields.

During the latter part of 2017, April and Laura reached another strategic decision. They agreed the two of them should relocate to Mozambique in January 2018. After working there for perhaps 12 to 18 months they would then return to their permanent base in Zambia, to carry on the coordination of HSC across Africa.

Several factors contributed to this decision. April wanted to give the new Zambia Hope on the Streets leaders more space; she was sensitive to the fact that within the African culture it was sometimes difficult for Alex and Janet Mulenga to have their area coordinator on base with them. Their natural inclination was to defer to her. However, an even more critical reason behind such a move was the urgency of reinforcing the work of Hope on the Streets in Mozambique. April wrote to prayer partners:

The OM training base in Mocuba is like the one in Zambia, but very understaffed and under-resourced. When we returned from our HSC training in Mozambique we started to mobilize people to go there and help. Sharon Kunda has responded, and so has Ephraim Zulu, but we expressed concerns to Africa Area Leader Melvin Chiombe about sending inexperienced people to set up a new department in a struggling field. While he was confident that we should move ahead and had great plans to build up this field, he too was concerned with the shortage of long-term OM people to mentor the team.

As we noticed some of the young HSC Zambia team members continually contacting us rather than Alex, and as we saw the situation in Mozambique, we started to pray more about whether we should move to that country for a time. It seemed clear to Laura and me, along with our leaders, families and churches, that God was directing us there.

He has graciously provided us with a partially furnished house to rent, which is owned by the church. It has sufficient grounds for us to grow our own vegetables. We are all studying Portuguese, as they do not speak English in Mozambique. The curriculum is being translated. Please pray for finances, strength and wisdom for each step of this move. Although it was very difficult to get a work and residential visa, the Lord is greater than the visa office!

And so began another chapter that is yet to be written.

In his book about children victimized by war, *One Day the Soldiers Came*, Charles London (2007) observed:

Children can survive without comforts – they are amazingly adaptable. They can survive without safety, even, drawing on what resources they have to get by, but they cannot long survive without hope. It is the job of every adult . . . to bend their minds to the task of giving hope, of creating a world where childhood can flourish, where play is possible.

Traumatized children who make it into adulthood continue to carry scars in their bodies and minds. The good and evil, love and hate that has shaped them into the people they have become has the potential to affect our world – and the future of millions more children. Not all of us can do what April Holden and her co-workers have chosen to undertake in obedience to the will of God. But we all have the capability of giving hope, and partnering with others through focused prayer and giving.

In God's great scheme of things, one of the boys rescued from probable death on the streets of North Africa by April and her team of hope-givers is now leading the work she was forced to leave behind. Recently he put his redemption story, mentioned in earlier chapters, into his own words.

My name is Jacob. When I was in the streets I became very sick indeed. I said to myself, 'If I stay here in the market I will die.'

One day Mama April came to me and took me to the Sisters of Mercy TB isolation hospital, where I stayed for many months. Then she took me to live at the Centre of Love. So I left what I was doing in the streets, like glue sniffing and sleeping under parked cars. I believe the opportunity was from our God. He sent someone from a far place to help the lost children and street boys and get them to a good life. I became known to God and am now happy indeed. I am alive! I know how to read and write. After I grew up in the centre I found work there as a teacher of small boys and help them still, like younger brothers.

I, Jacob, thank God so much, because He's done great things in my life. My thanks also to those who helped to bring hope to me and other brothers, and to the needy peoples of the world. I am asking my God always to bless the people who helped us, wherever they are, because we were completely lost in the streets before. Now most of us have become good people and members of churches.

And to my beloved Mama April Holden, may our God give you long life because He called you to help the street boys, taking them out of the market and joining them with other people. It's not easy, this calling from God. So thanks a lot, sweet Mama. You too are blessed.

Reflecting on the way that God, by His grace, has used Jacob to carry on the ministry she started in North Africa, April has to agree. She remembers the scores of other rescued boys who are now university graduates, accountants, pilots, pastors, professors, computer engineers and masters of other trades and professions; men leading rich, fulfilling lives as they care for families and serve the Lord with gladness. And her heart fills with thanksgiving that the paths of thousands more children across Africa can now take a different trajectory through the efforts of Hope on the Streets for Children.

A colossal challenge remains. Some 50 million children on our planet have been uprooted and torn from all that is familiar to them. Now they seek a safe place to call home. Although children make up about a third of the earth's population, they account for almost half of all refugees. There isn't a nation in the world that has no young people in need of rescue.

No doubt many will dismiss April Holden's vision for the Church to become the family of the fatherless, just as April herself was at first rejected as a candidate for missionary service over 30 years ago. But scoffers reckon without the One who has proven that although with man such a vision is impossible, with God all things are possible.

Mother Teresa (1995), who founded the Missionaries of Charity, shared a profound conclusion after years of experience with the destitute:

> The most terrible poverty is loneliness and the feeling of being unloved. The biggest disease today is not leprosy or tuberculosis, but rather the feeling of being unwanted. There is more hunger in the world for love and appreciation than for bread. We think sometimes that poverty is only being hungry, naked and homeless. The poverty of being unwanted, unloved and uncared for is the greatest poverty.

Yet God makes the formula for meeting this impoverishment very simple: *Receive love. Give love. Repeat.*

This famous missionary to India's outcasts maintained that we cannot do great things on this earth, only small things with great love. April would add that the relentless sort of love that is required must come from a Source beyond ourselves: 'The One most deserving of glory, honour and thanks for all the transformations made among Africa's children is God Himself. For it is His work, they are His children, and it is in His strength and by His grace that we do it. As they say in North Africa, '*La shukran ala wajib*' ('There is no need for thanks over duty done'). What a joy to go about our Father's business! And what a blessing to have a Father who is willing to have us work alongside Him, in spite of our weaknesses and mistakes!'

Postscript: partners are vital

Many people tend to put missionaries on a pedestal, especially those who pioneer or lead ministries. It is so easy to forget that it is all God's work and that many individuals are involved, each one as equally important as cogs powering a machine. If one is faulty the machine cannot function well. God offers all of us the privilege of lending our resources to get the job done.

Support team partners

Behind every missionary and every programme there is a team: finance officers, personnel and administration staff and those who handle financial development, IT and communications. The list could go on. Each person usually has responsibility for a variety of ministries. Their roles are vital to missionaries in the field. Yet support team members often struggle to raise their own financial backing.

Prayer and financial secretaries

My prayer secretaries, Mair Gray and more recently Karen Abbot, have faithfully worked and sacrificed part of their own income to send out my prayer letter. My aunt, Edna Holden, and then David Abbott, collected finance to send to the OM office for the ministry and my personal support. My sister, Susan Paton, has worked tirelessly, distributing letters, raising funds, doing presentations and collecting contributions.

Prayer partners

Our Father could act alone, but He has chosen to work through the intercession of His people. Prayer moves the hand of God, and those who approach Him in faith are those who bring success to the ministry. Besides members of my family I have been privileged to have prayer partners in many churches in the UK and across the globe. Many former OM workers are also spiritual partners. If I tried to name them all I would be sure to miss some.

Financial partners

As I look back over the years I clearly see how God has used people in countless countries to support me and my ministry. Friends in the United Kingdom include the United Reformed Church, Rainford; St John's Ravenhead, St Helens; Brook Lane Community Church, Bromley; All Saints Church, Rainford; Methodist Church Ladies Fellowship, Bicester; Orchard Baptist Church, Bicester; and the Mavis Harris prayer group. Added to these are regular contributions from dozens of individuals and members of churches in Germany, Hong Kong, the USA, Scotland and the rest of Britain, as well as many of my own family members and other friends such as the very generous 'M' family in London. I cannot name them all, nor would many of them wish any kind of public acknowledgement.

Still other men, women and even children have given time and effort in fund-raising for various projects. Alan and Margaret Abbott, for instance, obtained small boxes from a pharmaceutical company and pasted on photos of boys from the Centres of Love, to distribute to churches. Alan collected the boxes monthly and sent in the money for the boys, raising thousands of pounds over the years. An artist friend sold many paintings and raised £10,000 for our work. My mother's sister held an annual coffee morning as a fundraiser. Sunday school children from Brook Lane saved money for bricks by putting their pocket-money coins into Smarties boxes. And there were others who used their creative initiative.

In addition, we are thankful to have had income from large trust funds and foundations – two Scottish groups in particular that prefer to remain anonymous. Some gave one-off donations for building projects; other gifts have continued year in and year out, over decades.

God has seen it all, from the smallest child's coin to thousands of pounds from the biggest foundations, and valued each gift as vital to His plans for the vulnerable children of Africa.

Partner missions and cross-cultural volunteers

We are deeply appreciative of being able to work with groups such as Mission 21 and World Orphans for building (and monthly financing) the centres in North Africa. These partnerships enriched our work and indeed made it possible.

So did the many men and women who voluntarily came from Switzerland, South Korea, the USA, Canada, the UK, Sweden, Germany, the Netherlands, Malaysia, Kenya, South Africa and other countries to serve at the Centres of Love, for either short or long periods. Each one contributed skills that enriched the staff and children, whether it was carpentry, arts and crafts or other activities, medical help, agricultural expertise, administration, Bible teaching or staff training.

Local sustainability

We continually stress the importance of Christians on the ground, willing either to support projects started by expatriate workers or to pioneer their own. Mention of some of the national churches, groups and individuals who have generously given of themselves for the sake of Africa's street children has been integrated into the pages of this book.

Pastoral/friendship support

I will always be indebted to the many believers over the years who have offered me much-needed pastoral care and moral support. Some have emailed and skyped and some have personally visited. Without accountability to pastors and local churches, and the care and feeding given by counsellors and mentors, how quickly any of us can go astray. And without contact from family and friends, how soon we can wander into the valley of loneliness and discouragement.

I fear that in naming some individuals I have missed others, and risk offending some of the faithful. God knows the name of every person who was essential to the ministry through the years.

Are those who are not in the field less important than those who are? By no means! The work can make no progress without support from outside. Are the leaders of programmes more important than lay workers? Never! In the Lord's reckoning the project cook is just as valuable as the project head.

Your purchase of this book has already helped to further our efforts for vulnerable children. *Thank you!* Please check out our website at: <www.omafrica.org/hope-on-the-streets> and Facebook page: <www.facebook.com/hopeonthestreets>. If you feel that God is leading you to partner with us further, you can safely channel communications and contributions through your country's OM office, with the designation of 'Hope on the Streets for Children, Africa'. In the UK this address is: OM International, The Quinta, Weston Rhyn, Oswestry, Shropshire SY10 7LT.

April Holden

Notes

1 This county was later subdivided and St Helens became part of Merseyside.
2 Traditional wooden sailboat used on the Red Sea and eastern Mediterranean.
3 A superstitious fear of twins has existed historically in a number of African tribal cultures. One of the greatest achievements of nineteenth-century Scottish missionary to the Calabar in Nigeria, Mary Slessor, was stopping the killing of twins. Interestingly, other tribes, such as the Yoruba, on the contrary, attribute supernatural powers to twins and even worship them.
4 If you would like to learn more about kingdom building, loving your neighbours and caring about the vulnerable, you can visit <www.iambethwatkins.com> or download the free e-book at <www.iam-bethwatkins.com/e-book>.
5 See the report by the BBC for more information about child soldiers at: <www.bbc.com/news/world-africa-29762263>.
6 The Tabitha Initiative, part of Tabitha Skills Development, is a group that reaches out to parentless children and the HIV-ravaged population of South Africa (see <www.tabithaministries.org>).
7 See the four-minute OMNIvision video about how OM is working with Kayeye girls to empower them and offer them opportunities to do other work at: <https://vimeo.com/105783621>.

References and resources

Listed below are books referred to in the text and a selection of some of the excellent media available to help you get a clearer idea of what is happening with vulnerable children worldwide. The websites will also point you to ways in which you can help.

General

Ajak, Benjamin (2006) *They Poured Fire on Us From the Sky.* New York: Public Affairs.

Atiya, Nayra (1982) *Khul-Khaal: Five Egyptian women tell their story.* Syracuse, NY: Syracuse University Press.

Bixler, Mark (2005) *The Lost Boys of Sudan: An American story of the refugee experience.* Athens, GA: University of Georgia Press.

Butcher, Andy (1996) *Street Children: The tragedy and challenge of the world's millions of modern-day Oliver Twists.* Milton Keynes: Authentic Lifestyle.

Dallaire, Roméo (2010) *They Fight Like Soldiers, They Die Like Children: The global quest to eradicate the use of child soldiers.* New York: Random House.

Huang, Chi-Chen and Tang, Irwin (2006) *When Invisible Children Sing: A true story of five street children, an idealistic doctor and their dangerous hope.* Carol Stream, IL: Tyndale.

Klepp, Lillian Ann (2012) *Adventures Under the Mango Tree.* Maitland, FL: Xulon Press.

Lewis, C. S. (1966) *Surprised by Joy: The shape of my early life.* New York: Harcourt, Brace & World.

—— (1996) *The Joyful Christian.* New York: Touchstone, page 30.

Lomong, Lopez (2012) *Running for My Life: One lost boy's journey from the killing fields of Sudan to the Olympic Games.* Nashville, TN: Thomas Nelson.

London, Charles (2007) *One Day the Soldiers Came: Voices of children in war.* New York: Harper Perennial.

Mandryk, Jason (2010) *Operation World: The definitive prayer guide to every nation.* Nottingham: IVP.

Marlowe, Jen (2006) *Darfur Diaries: Stories of survival.* New York: Nation Books.

Perry, Michele (2009) *Love Has a Face: Mascara, a machete and one woman's miraculous journey with Jesus in Sudan*. Ada, MI: Chosen.

Salisbury, Saralyn (2012) 'The practice of ritual killings and human sacrifice in Africa', *Human Rights Brief*. Washington, DC: Center for Human Rights and Humanitarian Law, American University Washington College of Law. Available online at: <www.HRBrief.org/2012/09/the-practice-of-ritual-killings-and-human-sacrifice-in-africa>.

Teresa, Mother (1995) *A Simple Path*. New York: Ballantine Books.

Phyllis Kilbourn

In her training courses, April Holden uses the following titles that Phyllis Kilbourn authored, edited or contributed to (sometimes the books are compilations of contributions by different writers).

A Crisis Care Curriculum (April's main resource, composed of five modules: 'Trauma and crisis care', 'Street children', 'Care for orphans and vulnerable children', 'Children and soldiers', 'Train the trainer'). Fort Mill, SC: Crisis Care Training International.

Children Affected by HIV/AIDS: Crisis care. Wcl 3rd Party, 2002.

Children in Crisis: A new commitment. Wcl 3rd Party, 2013.

Healing for Hurting Hearts: A handbook for counselling children and youths in crisis. Fort Washington, PA: CLC Publications, 2013.

Healing the Children of War: A handbook for ministry to children who have suffered deep traumas. Wcl 3rd Party, 2013.

Let All the Children Come: A handbook for holistic ministry to children with disabilities. Fort Washington, PA: CLC Publications, 2013.

Sexually Exploited Children. Pasadena, CA: William Carey Library, 2013.

Shaping the Future: Girls and our destiny. Pasadena, CA: William Carey Library, 2008.

Street Children: A guide to effective ministry. Pasadena, CA: World Vision International, 1997.

Delving deeper

Leaf, Caroline (2009) *Who Switched Off My Brain? Controlling toxic thoughts and emotions*. Nashville, TN: Thomas Nelson. (April's team uses notes adapted from this book, with the author's permission.)

McDonald, Patrick and Garrow, Emma (2000) *Children at Risk: Networks in action*. Pasadena, CA: World Vision International.

Miles, Glenn and Wright, Josephine Joy (eds) (2004) *Celebrating Children: Equipping people working with children and young people living in difficult circumstances around the world*. Milton Keynes: Paternoster.

Williams, Andrew (2011) *Working with Street Children: An approach explored*. Lyme Regis, Dorset: Russell House.

Websites

Child soldiers/war victims

Child Soldiers International
www.child-soldiers.org

Child Victims of War
http://childvictimsofwar.org.uk

Save the Children
www.savethechildren.org

War Child
www.warchild.org

Children and HIV or AIDS

AIDSLink International
www.aidslinkinternational.org

Avert
www.avert.org/professionals/hiv-social-issues/key-affected-populations/
children

Street kids, abuse, poverty

Children International
www.children.org

Consortium for Street Children
http://streetchildren.org

Every Child Ministries
www.ecmafrica.org

Hope on the Streets
www.omafrica.org/hope-on-the-streets (Facebook: www.facebook.com/
hopeonthestreets/)

International Day for Street Children (12 April)
www.streetchildrenday.org

International Street Kids
www.internationalstreetkids.com

KidsRights Foundation
https://kidsrights.org/action

Toybox
https://toybox.org.uk

Viva – Together for Children
www.viva.org

WomenAid Children of the World Initiative
www.womenaid.org/wcwi.htm

World Vision
www.worldvision.org

Trafficking

ECPAT International (End Child Prostitution, Pornography and Trafficking of Children for Sexual Purposes)
www.ecpat.org

Not for Sale
www.notforsalecampaign.org

Stop the Traffik
www.stopthetraffik.org